MOUSECATRAZ

MOUSECATRAZ

The Disney College Program

Wesley Jones
with
Michael Esola

MP

Mantra Press
A Division of Mantra Hospitality, LLC.

Mousecatraz: The Disney College Program

Cover art by Scott Washington and Katherine Gray

Copyright © 2010 by Mantra Press
Second Edition
All rights reserved

ISBN: 978-0-578-05813-9

Printed in the United States of America

For more information regarding future titles and consulting services, please visit www.MantraHospitality.com

To the Disney College Program cast members,
whose dedication to the Disney dream is immeasurable

Contents

Introduction
Mousecatraz: The Place

Introduction

In 2006 when I completed the first edition of *Mousecatraz: The Walt Disney World College Program*, I wanted to achieve something that had yet to be accomplished, to provide an indepth insight into a remarkable internship experience like none other in the world. Since releasing the first edition, thousands of copies sold and along with that came great praise for daring to uncover what is an unforgettable experience where anything is possible. Along with that praise came criticism that suggested that many of the experiences discussed within *Mousecatraz* could no way occur in a million years. For those die-hard college program students who have experienced similar events, they know what I'm talking about. Anything is possible at Disney! And what happens behind the walls of Mousecatraz can widen many eyes in disbelief.

Other readers believed that the first edition provided a negative connotation to the Disney College Program. This was most certainly not intended. I wanted a balance of the good and, the bad, and with the second edition that same balance holds true. Let me go on record right now and say that I applaud the Disney College Program and every experience associated with it.

This program has both positive and negative qualities, but which company program doesn't have those. I encourage anyone reading this who isn't a program alum to consider applying. It will change your life in so many positive ways that no other company could provide.

The Walt Disney World College Program in Orlando, Florida, and Disneyland Resort College Program in Anaheim, California, are both a unique experience unknown to most college students, Walt Disney World Resort and Disneyland Resort guests, and Disney fanatics from all over the world. Designed as a four to six month program for qualified college students, the once-in-a-lifetime internship provides students with a *Living, Learning,* and *Earning* experience. Many unique experiences occur during a student's internship with the Walt Disney World Resort and Disneyland Resort: good, bad, serious, funny, unbelievable, outrageous, and even unimaginable. These experiences have never been explored, up until now.

For over four years I researched the myths, stories, and legends that took place in the Disney College Program. My research began in August, 2003, when I participated in the College Program. I lived, learned and earned like every other student in the program. I worked in Main Street U.S.A. Daily Operations at the Magic Kingdom, lived in a two-bedroom wellness apartment with three roommates at Vista Way, and took one education course during my internship.

Following my five-month experience of participating in the program, I moved forward with the four-year research process by conducting interviews of past and present Disney College Program students. I was able to uncover thousands of stories from over eight hundred interviews and discussions. The purpose of these stories and research findings aren't to discourage potential candidates about participating in the program, but to inform and entertain readers about the incredible and memorable adventures that take place in this unique program.

The official internship title is *College Program Cast Member*. For the purposes of this book, I refer to the title as *College Program Student* and regular employees at the Walt Disney World Resort as the traditional *Disney Speak* term, *Cast Member*.

Detailed information regarding Disney College Program student requirements, expectations, benefits, Walt Disney World Resort and Disneyland Resort job descriptions, and Disney College Program class descriptions have been obtained from the Disney College Program's official website, www.wdwcollegeprogram.com.

This book is not all about the Walt Disney World Resort or Disneyland Resort, but about an internship experience unlike any other in the world. I may have participated in the College Program to help confirm and secure a large percentage of my research, but this book is not about me nor is it really my book. These are the adventures and experiences of past Disney College Program students.

Mousecatraz: The Place

Mousecatraz is the common term tossed around among Disney cast members when describing the Disney College Program. The term is derived from Alcatraz Island, a former federal prison located in the middle of the San Francisco Bay. Students describe the Disney College Program with the "Mousecatraz" title because of the tight security presence in student housing, long hours at the Mouse house, and the institutionalized environment that most students experience. The "Mousecatraz" title is in no way suggesting that Disney property is a bad place to live, work or play. Many students will choose to live at Mousecatraz any day, and, I would have to agree with them! Then again, you can come to your own conclusions and decide what Mousecatraz is really like.

Can you survive Mousecatraz?

Chapter One

Calling All Students

I do not want to make teaching films. If I did, I would create a separate organization. It is not higher education that interests me so much as general mass education.
—Walt Disney

Playboy.com calls the Disney College Program one of the sexiest internships in which to participate. How could an internship possibly be sexy? Is it because that over two thousand college-aged students live in very tight quarters? Doubtful. Is it because of the lederhosen the students are required to wear in Germany at Epcot? Probably not. Is it because of the late night parties and two hours of sleep that exist before students wake up at 5:00 A.M. to open the theme parks? Possibly. Maybe the real reason the College Program is one of the sexiest internships in which to participate is because of the magical pixie dust and oversized mouse ears. Whatever the reason for this title, the spicy truth about the Disney College Program will be revealed in the following pages as seen through the eyes of those who have experienced it. Then you can decide for yourself why this unique program is called one of the sexiest internships in which a person can participate.

The Disney College Program started from humble beginnings employing just over two hundred students from thirty colleges and universities in 1981. In the following twenty-nine years, the College Program would grow beyond belief, employing more than sixty thousand students from nations all over the globe. The numbers continue to grow each year as the program welcomes new and eager students ready to begin a journey that will change their lives forever.

The Walt Disney World Resort recruits students for an internship experience in what the company calls a *Living*, *Learning*, and *Earning* experience. Students from a variety of college majors may apply. Some of the few majors include Business Administration, Communication, Liberal Arts, and Sport Management. Students who have undecided majors can apply as well. Essentially, any warm body in college may apply. Students may choose to apply for a five to six month fall or spring session, a summer session (available to College Program alumni only; yes, many students do return!), or a six to eight month extended fall or spring session, referred to as the fall or spring advantage program.

Interested candidates must be enrolled at a college or university part-time or full-time. Good academic standing is required, which includes a cumulative grade point average of 2.0. The College Program is one of the few internship programs that allows students to receive both pay and college credit for their hard work (credited through the American Council on Education). Pay and college credit for an internship is unheard of in most internship programs, but the overall value of the College

Program is far greater than a transcript notation or a weekly paycheck with the Mouse's imprint.

Over the years, the College Program has grown and some changes have been implemented. In 2005, the Walt Disney World College Program's official title was changed to the Disney Theme Parks & Resorts College Program. The company believed changing the program's title strategically positioned the College Program for synergy purposes. This was a sensible business move, yet most past, present, and even future College Program participants will continue referring to their experiences in the program by its original title.

The College Program began offering what the company calls a "career start" to a high school graduate's future. To be eligible, a student must have earned a high school diploma or GED within the last eighteen months of applying and be at least eighteen years old when his or her program begins. Behind the fancy wording, this new program is really no different than the original Disney College Program. Clever marketing strategies by the company's *MarketEARs* have reached out in an attempt to meet the resort's increasing demand for labor, yet keeping their payroll manageable. This approach is a smart move, and high school students who have recently graduated, but are unaware of what career path they want to take, should consider applying.

Disney International Programs offer opportunities for students living outside of the United States of America. Students can participate in a summer work experience while on a J-1 training visa for a maximum of ninety days. Some of the students who have participated in the program have come from locations such as Hong Kong, Brazil, Peru, and Canada just to name a few. Students can also apply for a twelve month Cultural Representative Program where they'll most likely be stationed at Epcot's World Showcase.

Disney Professional Internships are offered to non-alumni, but there are selected professional internships that are available to alumni only. Professional internships are typically six months in length but can last longer depending on the role. Students have the opportunity to work in finance, human resources, operations, transportation, and sales just to name a few. The professional internships can be a great opportunity for students to get their foot in the door and obtain a full-time status with the company.

~

Candidates typically find out about the College Program in the simplest ways. There are the students who walk by those colorful yellow flyers or posters plastered all over their college campus. There are those who hear their peers talking about wanting to work at the Walt Disney World Resort or Disneyland Resort. Finally, there are the select few who come across the program in the most peculiar ways.

After getting pulled over by California Highway Patrol, a speeding candidate looked for his proof of vehicle insurance in his vehicle's storage compartment. Instead, he came across a small, yellow flyer advertising the College Program and, out of curiosity, pulled it out. The proof of vehicle insurance wasn't found, and the candidate's license was suspended for a short duration. Luckily for the candidate it didn't matter because he decided to apply and was accepted into the program. He didn't have to worry about driving for an entire year. This student went on to work at the Magic Kingdom's Tomorrowland Indy Speedway. After enjoying a successful four month program, he returned to his undergraduate studies and to the real California freeways.

Another candidate learned about the program through her counselor, and both she and her counselor attended a campus presentation about the program. The counselor had negative thoughts about the program prior to the campus presentation. After the presentation concluded, the counselor's student declined an interview, but the counselor eagerly applied without hesitation. Unfortunately for the counselor, she wasn't accepted into the program. She re-applied the following year and was accepted to work as a Vacation Planner.

Some candidates come across the College Program just by walking on their college campus. Not paying attention to where he was walking, the 4.0 candidate walked straight into a light pole. Ironically, he smacked his face into a program flyer that informed students of a campus presentation. The presentation was minutes from starting and after shoving pieces of tissue up his bloody nose, the injured candidate attended. The student accepted a role at the Magic Kingdom as a Custodial Host. After one month in the program, he realized that his 4.0 grade point average would be more valuable. Hopefully, he made the right decision.

One candidate walked past an information booth advertising the College Program. The candidate asked the campus representative sitting at the table, wearing mouse ears and a nametag, if he worked at Walt Disney World. The representative explained that he worked at Walt Disney World while in the College Program. The candidate asked, "So, can I get an internship with Universal Studios?" The student wasn't offered a role with the program.

Many candidates come across the College Program by mistake. One lost candidate interrupted a campus presentation and asked the program recruiter where the university had moved his elementary algebra class. Once informed his class wasn't relocated nor simply wasn't scheduled, the candidate engaged in an argument with the recruiter. After calming down, he took a seat, listened to the presentation and applied. First impressions are lasting and this particular candidate wasn't hired.

After a campus presentation concluded, a confused candidate was exiting the room and asked the program recruiter how he would receive his $10. The recruiter explained there never was any announcement of receiving compensation for attending the presentation. A nearby candidate overhearing the conversation interrupted and explained that the research experiment paying $10 for participation was located in the next room. The lost candidate applied and was accepted into the program.

Several candidates learn about the College Program through their current employers, but sometimes through the most unusual circumstances. While working during one fall at Disneyland in Anaheim, California, a student engaged in an argument with his manager. The frustrated manager didn't want to terminate the student but didn't want to work with him either. The manager came up with an idea and suggested to the student that he try out the College Program at Walt Disney World. The student welcomed the suggestion and participated in the program. Ironically, the manager transferred to Florida six months later and was, once again, the student's manager.

During one particular fall a young employee was terminated for being intoxicated while working at Six Flags in Texas. Before the employee vacated the park, his supervisor said, "Go apply for Disney World's College Program." The terminated employee applied and was offered an internship. To no one's surprise the student was terminated from the program for drinking in a wellness apartment at Vista Way apartments.

After a candidate was terminated from the Disneyland Resort for poor attendance, he asked his manager, "Do you think I could get a job at Walt Disney World?" The manager replied, "Try applying in twelve months. They may take you." The candidate applied twelve months later and didn't get into the program.

One smelly candidate learned about the College Program while digging through a garbage dumpster on his college campus. The candidate mistakenly threw a term paper in the garbage, and the important document ended up in a larger dumpster downstairs. While searching through several bags of garbage, the candidate came across a small yellow flyer with a drawing of Mickey Mouse's ears. Intrigued, the candidate attended a campus presentation and the rest was history. Ironically, the student worked as a Custodial Host while in the program. When asked how he found out about the program, he would answer, "In the garbage."

A Fall, 2004 alumnus recalls: "I was in the library before a big test and needed a sheet of paper to write the answers onto so I could use it during my test. I went to class and during the test, I pulled out that sheet, only to discover the front side was an advertisement for the College Program. It looked cool and I was hooked. The only problem was that the professor caught me looking at the flyer with the answers on the back. All I could say was the flyer wasn't mine. The professor failed me for the class, but I was lucky enough not to get kicked out of school. I look back and realize the 'Mouse' almost got me kicked out of school."

A Spring, 2005 alumnus remembers: "My girlfriend dumped me, gave me a College Program flyer and said, 'Here, go do something with your life!' In the end, she did me a favor."

A Spring, 2009 alumnus advises, "Do yourself a favor and apply for the program. It will be the best decision of your life!"

~

After candidates obtain more information about the College Program, they're encouraged to attend a campus presentation at their college or a nearby college. Up until recently, every candidate was required to attend a presentation in-person. Today, presentations can be given daily on-line in lieu of in-person. During the presentation, recruiters and campus representatives provide an overview of what the program has to offer. Student testimonials through video segments reveal how the program changed their lives forever. The common phrase of "It's the Journey that Changed Me" sticks with candidates as the theme song to "It's a Small World" sticks with its riders.

Campus presentations can bring out the most interesting questions from candidates. During one presentation, a six-foot tall candidate asked if he could play Mickey Mouse. The recruiter explained that Disney required a shorter person to play Mickey Mouse. The puzzled candidate asked, "So, why can't I play Mickey Mouse?" The candidate was offered a role in Food and Beverage. He went on to obtain a Professional Internship from the Walt Disney World Resort.

Another candidate asked why he had to listen to a presentation about the Walt Disney World Resort. The inquiring candidate was a bit confused as he thought the program took place at Disneyland Paris. After the recruiter helped the candidate understand the details, the candidate declined to interview.

A rather odd candidate asked if she could bring her pet rat with her if she was chosen to participate. After the recruiter explained the policies and declined her request, the candidate said, "That's ridiculous. Mickey's a rat, so why can't I bring my rat?" The candidate immediately got up from her chair and left the presentation.

Some campus presentations bring out the bold candidates in the room. One candidate raised her hand and asked, "Will there be a test on what we just learned?" The recruiter explained that no test would be given. The confused candidate said, "Good, I wasn't paying attention. It was boring." This uninterested candidate declined an interview and went on to work for a canning factory, which is probably much more interesting than Disney. Well, maybe not.

During another presentation, a candidate interrupted and asked how big the Walt Disney World Resort is in size. The recruiter explained it over forty-three square miles. The candidate responded, "That's it? That's not very big. Not interested."

A particularly intrigued candidate wanted to know what the percentage rate for sex was while in the program. The perplexed recruiter explained that she didn't have that information. The brave candidate asked, "So, how many times did you have sex while in the program?" The recruiter declined to answer the inappropriate question. The candidate applied but wasn't offered a role.

A Spring, 2003 alumnus remembers: "The recruiters Mouse-Washed us in forty-five minutes. I thought to myself this could be the time of my life, but also knew there'd be no way in hell I'd ever be offered an interview with my qualifications. I was only eighteen, had no experience, only six college units at the community college, and no personal skills. Then the recruiter asked me if I wanted an interview. Without hesitation, I said yes! It was the best decision I've ever made."

A Fall, 2003 alumnus reveals his interview strategy: "I knew there'd be group interviews of five or six. I brought five friends with me to the presentation that didn't want the internship. We all scheduled an interview for the following morning. Obviously, they didn't show up and it was a one-on-one interview. I got the work location, desired role, and living location I requested."

A Spring, 2008 alumnus recalls: "I viewed the online campus presentation and was thinking that this would be the greatest opportunity in the world. At the end of the presentation, I got a phone call from a company, not Disney, and they offered me a full-time job. I said no thanks; I'm going to Disney World!"

~

After campus presentations conclude, candidates can sign up for an on-site group interview. How could a candidate not want to sign up? The smiling faces explaining the benefits of the warm Florida sunshine are tough to resist for any young student fresh out of high school or early in his or her college career. Candidates attending presentations in-person always crowd around the recruiters after the forty-five minute spiel concludes. Do candidates really know what they're getting themselves into? Do they expect to play in the theme parks everyday? Do they not understand they have to work? Candidates rarely inquire about the dirty details such as the long hours, low pay, and tight living conditions. All that is thought about is the pixie dust and the magic with which each candidate grew up.

Disney interviews are similar to any other job interview, but interviewees quickly discover one slight difference. Group interviews consisting of three to four eager candidates are conducted. Several important elements such as a smile, group interaction, and enthusiasm must be demonstrated. Most of the interview questions are short, simple, and to-the-point. Even though each interview varies, common questions consist of past experience, group projects, interest in Disney, and even whether or not a candidate has any visible tattoos.

Whether interviews are conducted on-site or via telephone, several things can go wrong with candidates' interviews. One candidate wasn't thinking about what she was saying and indicated that she would do anything possible to get the internship. The recruiter thought her answer was inappropriate and didn't offer her a role.

Another candidate had her wisdom teeth removed the day before her interview. With a mouth full of gauze and looking like a chipmunk, the candidate smiled, only to lose her bloody gauze out of her mouth and onto the table. She grabbed the gauze, shoved it into her pocket, and answered the interview questions. She was offered a role as a ticket taker because the recruiter liked her smile, or so she thinks.

Enthusiasm is one important quality for which recruiters look, but some candidates can go above and beyond. One enthusiastic candidate was so energetic that another candidate in the group directly asked if she had A.D.D. The energetic candidate informed the group that she didn't have the disease, but was "doped up on Disney." It's unknown whether the candidate asking the question was offered a role, but the candidate on "Disney drugs" was offered a role at the Magic Kingdom as a Character Attendant.

During a memorable group interview, two candidates engaged in an argument over who knew more about Disney. At the end of the heated argument, both candidates assumed Walt Disney was still alive and asked if they'd be able to meet him during the program. The recruiter explained that they were mistaking Walt's nephew Roy for Walt himself. One of the students asked, "Who's Roy?"

While not necessary, it's beneficial to find common ground with the recruiter. In one interview, the recruiter learned that one of the candidates was a Resident Assistant. Having been a R.A. herself, the two engaged in a conversation about stories of the R.A. position. After a twenty-minute discussion, the sidetracked recruiter remembered there were still two other candidates in the interview. The R.A. candidate was offered a role in Food & Beverage.

Most candidates hope to get their first choices in a job role, but it's important to remember that honesty is always the best policy. During one interview, a candidate using crutches informed the recruiter she couldn't work at a location where she'd be required to stand. The recruiter explained it wouldn't be an issue and described some of the alternative opportunities. The interview concluded and apparently the candidate was so excited, she forgot that she was faking the injury in order for her request to be granted. The healthy candidate got up from the table and walked out of the room, leaving her crutches behind. Interestingly, the dishonest candidate was hired and placed in a ticket-taker role where standing was required. She left the program after her first two weeks.

Sometimes it's best for candidates not to display certain areas of their body when the topic of tattoos is addressed. One candidate pulled up his shirtsleeve to reveal a tattoo of a naked woman. The candidate was hired but placed in a backstage role away from park guests.

During an interview with the recruiter and four other candidates, a candidate revealed his three tattoos to the shocked group and proceeded to show a fourth tattoo in an unusual location. To the group's surprise, Mickey and Minnie Mouse were tattooed on his butt, Mickey on one side and Minnie on the other. The candidate didn't get an offer from the company.

Different interests in Disney lead a candidate to apply for the College Program. One candidate was asked about his interest in the College Program. The confident candidate explained there was no interest but heard the College Program was an easy place to get laid. The candidate wasn't offered a role with the company.

Another candidate described her interest in Disney as being her religion and that she worshiped the company and everything it stood for. To her, Mickey Mouse was God on Earth. The recruiter was a little concerned and decided that it was in the company's best interest to not provide an offer to this student.

It can be beneficial for candidates to think of possible responses to questions before going into any interview. An honest candidate described one of the past group projects in which he participated as a great success, but the project was during a four-month sentence at the local jail. Even though he was honest, he wasn't offered a role.

A sexually active candidate described a past job experience as enriching and enjoyable because of the beautiful girls with whom he had sexual relationships. This candidate would have fit in nicely with the Vista Way culture, but, unfortunately for him he didn't get accepted into the program.

At times it can be smart for candidates to keep their opinions to themselves during the interview. After explaining The Walt Disney Company was to be in her long-term career plans, a candidate indicated she would leave the College Program after she used the company for the experience. She never got the opportunity to enhance her resume.

Another candidate concluded her interview by asking if Universal Studios Orlando offered a program equivalent to the Disney College Program. The recruiter explained there was no similar program and the candidate said, "That's too bad. I'm sure they'd pay more." This candidate never got to experience the Disney pay.

During one interview, a candidate was asked to explain a two-year gap in her employment history. The candidate explained she was terminated from nine jobs during this given time period, so she believed it would be best to leave her employment history blank. She didn't have the opportunity to make Disney her tenth job in two years.

To add to the job hopper list, a candidate described his past experiences as working for Warner Brothers, Universal, and Paramount. When asked why he wanted to gain experience at Disney, the candidate explained it was because all three companies had terminated him for stealing, and he wanted to try his luck at Disney. His luck must have run out because Disney wasn't willing to take a chance on him.

Two questions of importance asked during the interview are whether candidates plan to bring a car and how candidates feel about sharing an apartment with three to five other students. These fairly simple questions can lead to an interesting array of other questions and comments. One candidate asked if Disney provided students with an automobile and after the program concluded, if they're allowed to keep the automobile. The student wasn't given an automobile, and he had to ride the Disney-provided transportation to work.

Another candidate inquired if Disney would pay his car insurance if he brought his vehicle with him. After the recruiter responded with the obvious answer of no, the candidate got up and left the interview.

During one interview, a candidate indicated he didn't mind sharing an apartment with other students as long as he was designated the leader of the apartment. The candidate was offered a role in Attractions, and he got the opportunity to work on his team-building skills.

An unusual candidate didn't want to share an apartment with people he didn't know. After listening to the explanation that living with others was a large part of the program, the candidate asked if Disney would house him in an apartment off Disney property. The candidate's request wasn't granted nor was he offered an internship.

One spoiled candidate indicated he would only accept an internship if his apartment was furnished with a High-Definition television. The recruiter declined the request, and the needy candidate asked, "What about a wide-screen television instead?" He probably should have applied at an electronics store because Disney didn't believe that he'd be a good fit.

A Spring, 1999 alumna remembers: "A guy sitting next to me asked what the average number of students in the program that get terminated was. The recruiter didn't know the statistics. The guy asking the question said he needed to know so he'd know what his chances of getting terminated would be."

A Fall, 1999 alumnus recalls: "One guy in our group interview said he didn't mind sharing an apartment with other students but mentioned he had trouble getting along with others. He said he broke his last roommate's nose."

A Spring, 2002 candidate suggests: "Turn your cell phone off for the interview. My phone rang during the interview, and I answered it. Making matters worse, I left the room to continue with the phone conversation. I was eighteen, young, stupid, and immature. I should have never taken that call from my girlfriend who dumped me over the phone during my College Program interview."

A Fall, 2004 alumna recalls: "During my group interview, the recruiter asked what my past experiences involved and I told them Six Flags Magic Mountain. Another candidate in the interview interrupted and said, 'They're a better company to work for. They have better rides.' I highly doubt she was offered an internship."

A Spring, 2005 alumnus remembers: "I had my phone interview via my cell phone while driving on the 405 San Diego freeway. I was asked to describe a situation where I performed superior guest service. A truck cut me off, I yelled 'Effin asshole,' and continued with my answer. I don't know how it happened, but I got the internship."

Another Spring, 2005 alumnus recalls: "I was sitting in my parked car during my phone interview and suddenly got rear-ended by a truck. I got out of my car and approached the other driver. I said a few choice words, all while the recruiter was on the other line. I still got the job and am unaware of how my 'choice words' didn't make me look bad."

~

Candidates should always obtain their recruiter's contact information and immediately after the interview, complete a thank you letter. Following up with a thank you letter increases the chances for acceptance into the program. Candidates must show that they're not just warm bodies to fill a role but eager and professional candidates who are the right choice.

Sometimes a thank you letter isn't always wise. One candidate mailed a thank you letter that explained he was no longer interested in the internship. He believed working for a mouse was unethical.

A candidate mailed a thank you letter to her recruiter but misspelled half of the words, including the recruiter's name. A few days later, the candidate received a rejection letter. The candidate contacted the recruiter and asked why she wasn't accepted. The recruiter explained that all roles had been filled.

Another candidate, having spelling and grammar problems, mailed a thank you letter and spelled Disney as "Dizney" every time the word was used. The candidate never got the opportunity to see how Disney was spelled on her paycheck.

Utilizing email as a quicker method in sending a thank you letter to his recruiter, a young male candidate learned a valuable lesson. The candidate mistakenly attached a file which contained pictures of nude women. The candidate probably would have been offered an internship but received a rejection letter a few weeks later.

A Fall, 1998 alumna recalls: "I obtained my recruiter's mailing information and sent a few letters. I was using the wrong address and some old lady in Lake Buena Vista, Florida, was receiving my letters about the College Program."

~

A few weeks, sometimes months, may pass before candidates are notified of a decision. Candidates accepted into the program need to decide whether to accept or decline. A candidate choosing not to accept should always reply because it's a professional offer. A candidate choosing to accept is required to confirm the acceptance and an arrival date via the invitation. There are always a few candidates each year accepted into the program that either forget to accept the internship offer or accept the offer past the deadline date.

One forgetful candidate was positive she accepted her internship offer before the appropriate deadline. The candidate packed her bags, drove her car clear across the country from Oregon, and arrived at the check-in station at the Vista Way housing complex. To the candidate's surprise, she not only missed the acceptance deadline date but also forgot to accept her internship offer. Breaking down into tears and explaining her odd situation to program personnel, she was eventually allowed into the program.

Another candidate was offered an internship but decided not to accept the offer and didn't notify program personnel. The unprofessional candidate decided to reapply in the following year but was rejected immediately because of her actions, or lack of actions, during the previous year.

In a rather odd situation, one Fall, 2002 candidate believed her program began in Spring, 2003. The confused candidate arrived at the check-in station four months past her scheduled arrival date. After hours of phone calls and paperwork, she was offered a role for the Spring, 2003 program. Strangely, she declined and returned home.

A Fall, 2004 alumna recalls: "The moment I received my internship offer for Fall, 2003, I accepted the internship without thinking. Two weeks later, I remembered that I couldn't participate in the program until a year later. I got excited and forgot what I was doing."

~

Students prepare no differently than if they were going off to a traditional college campus to live. Some colleges require additional assignments to be completed during a student's stay in the program. Proper addresses and contact information on where to mail the assignments should be obtained. Students should also check on their car insurance (if taking an automobile), medical insurance, and, more importantly, make sure all of the paperwork is in order at their college's administrative offices. Some students, however, experience difficulties in completing such tasks.

One University of Michigan student was expecting to receive college credit for the program but forgot to complete the necessary paperwork required to obtain credit. The unlucky student was failed for the semester during which she participated in the program.

Another student completed his paperwork for the university he attended but was unaware of whom his direct supervisor would be while in the program. Instead of contacting program personnel, he just listed "Mickey Mouse" as his immediate supervisor.

A Fall, 1994 alumna remembers: "I finished my assignments and mailed them to my campus. The assignments were mailed to the Agriculture Department instead of the intended Political Science Department. The Agriculture Department was curious as to why they received something from Disney and tossed it into the garbage. I received an 'F' for my work until the situation could be straightened out nine months later."

~

Blue shorts or black shorts? T-shirts, dress shirts, long sleeve shirts, or collared shirts? Maybe some flip flops, a bathing suit and a beach towel? After all, it's sunny Florida. Packing clothing seems simple to most students, but it can be more complicated than one might imagine. Florida is hot, humid, and wet. Spring and summer students should bring cool clothing as it's hot all day and all night. Fall students should bring cool clothing, but also understand that Florida's popular climate does change as it can become cold during the winter months.

Packing the appropriate clothing can be difficult for some students, but most attempt their best at accomplishing such a task. A fall student from Canada packed nothing but warm clothing, and when she arrived, a new and cooler wardrobe needed to be purchased. After $200 was spent the student needed her parents to wire money to her bank account.

During one student's fall program, the temperature dropped well below thirty degrees during a late evening. Completely caught by surprise, the student needed to borrow warmer clothing from the Magic Kingdom's wardrobe department. A Security Hostess stopped the student at the bus entrance, and it was back to shorts and a t-shirt.

Another student packed all of his clothing, arrived and realized he forgot to pack his underwear. The surprised student decided not to borrow his roommate's underwear and quickly made a trip to the local Wal-Mart.

A well-packed student brought seven pieces of luggage with her on the plane. After arriving at Orlando International Airport in Florida, five of the seven pieces of luggage didn't arrive with her. The five pieces of luggage were never recovered and disappeared forever.

One clever student folded and packed his $3,000 Armani suit in his suitcase. After arriving in Florida, he opened his suitcase and discovered the suit was wrinkled and ripped. He questioned his new roommates, "How did this happen?"

Once clothing is packed into suitcases, the next obstacle to overcome is getting the luggage into the Orlando area. In a rather odd incident, one student drove to Florida with his luggage loaded in the back of his truck. With only sixty miles remaining until the student arrived in the Orlando area, he stopped at a rest area to take a quick nap. After a twenty minute nap, he continued his journey on the Florida roadways. A few miles down the road, the tired student glanced in his rear-view mirror and noticed something different about the back of his truck. To the student's surprise, his luggage had been stolen. About twenty miles outside of Orlando, the student pulled into a gas station. While filling his truck up with gasoline, he recognized his luggage sitting in the backseat of the car in front of him. After a phone call to the police and one hour later, the ironic situation grew larger. The clever thief was on his way to the Walt Disney World Resort where he was to participate in the College Program. Fortunately for Disney, the thief never made it to Disney property as he was arrested for a parole violation.

In a separate incident pertaining to luggage, two students drove to Florida together and made a stop about one hundred miles away from the Orlando area. After getting out of the vehicle, they discovered their luggage had fallen off the top of their vehicle. The two students searched the roadways they previously traveled, but the luggage was nowhere to be found.

A Fall, 2003 alumnus recalls: "My sister and I flew out of the same airport but to different locations. To this date I'm still unsure how it happened, but when I arrived I had my sister's suitcase. It took a few days for my suitcase to get to me in Florida."

A Spring, 2006 alumnus remembers: "I placed my black suitcase on the bed, opened it, and discovered it wasn't my suitcase. I was never able to get my luggage back. I couldn't do much with women's clothing."

~

Students are encouraged to bring money that will help get them started. After all, it will be a week or two before students receive a paycheck from the Mouse. Even worse, the paycheck isn't very large after rent and taxes are taken out. Recently, Disney began charging a non-refundable $100 fee due when accepting a program offer. The fee is referred to as a "Program Assessment & Activities Fee." Some students have made the argument that this is indeed not a paid internship but the other way around: "We pay Disney to become an intern." It's important to remember that Disney coordinates a series of live events for students while in the program, and these memorable events create great memories for all students who participate. Take advantage of every event possible. Students will realize that the $100 is well worth it.

Money management is always the first lesson that students learn while in the program. After spending $1,000 during her first night, a spoiled student called home asking for more money. Her parents wired $1,000 the following day. All $1,000 was spent before the evening concluded. After calling home yet again, another $1,000 was wired. The money was spent after two days, and a total of $3,000 was spent on Disney souvenirs. The parents learned their lesson and didn't wire any more money when their daughter requested another $1,000 two days later. The student finally learned how to manage her finances on a tight budget. She now works in accounting for a major retail organization on the West coast.

During one student's first day in Florida, all $1,000 she brought with her was spent during a thirty minute shopping spree in Downtown Disney. The bags full of sweatshirts, hats and other souvenirs were lost on a bus ride to Epcot.

Another student brought $500 in cash but lost all of it during his first night. Either one lucky person made some extra cash or the bottom of a garbage can got very lucky.

Instead of losing money or carelessly spending it, one lucky student received a nice surprise. On his first day and going for his wallet, the student discovered that his parents placed ten $100 bills in his billfold. Attached was a note stating, "Have the time of your life. Love, Mom and Dad."

A Fall, 2004 alumna states: "Disney might as well have paid us with cheap peanuts because the interns are slave labor. I needed my parents to wire me money just to make it through the first two months."

~

Some of the personal items that students bring with them include televisions, video games, Dolby Digital Surround Sound systems, miniature refrigerators, barbecues, fish tanks, and computers or laptops. Some items are a little overboard while other personal belongings just have no place while participating in the program.

A list is provided by Disney to help with the packing process, but some students believe they're above such summer camp lists. Not aware of the Florida climate, one student brought his sled with him. With no place to put the large sled, he stored it on his bed. Apparently, the sled was more important because the student slept on the floor for two weeks until he was able to sell it to a local resident.

One fall, three students from Colorado brought their snowboards. Perhaps they should have connected with the student who brought his sled.

A heavy-packing student brought every shoe she owned and a shoe rack to keep them all organized. Someone should have explained to her that sixty pairs of shoes weren't necessary for a four-month program.

A student from Montana brought his dirt bike and while trying to impress a couple of attractive female students, he ran his bike into a nearby pond on housing property. The student was okay, but the bike's motor needed some work.

One student brought his Pit Bull and before security could get the dog off property, the dog chased down two international students and left teeth marks in their legs. No rabies shots were needed, and the international students were okay.

Some students smuggle illegal items onto the property, or at least attempt to. One student brought two marijuana plants which were placed in his apartment's bathroom. After two months of growing the plants in the bathroom, a surprise room inspection was conducted, and all four students occupying the apartment were terminated from the program.

A rather strange student brought his collection of axes. His three roommates immediately requested to move to a new location. After their requests were granted, the strange student quit the program.

Another student brought his shotgun collection and was foolish enough to display it to a group of cast members assisting with the check-in procedure. The student didn't go any further and quit the program on the first day.

A Fall, 2000 alumna remembers: "My roommate brought a large living Christmas tree with her, and it was only August. She didn't think Florida had Christmas trees and she didn't want to be without one for Christmas."

A Spring, 2006 alumna recalls: "My roommate brought four televisions, two computers, and one laptop. She needed a television in the bathroom, bedroom, living room, and kitchen. When she was home, every television had to be turned on at all times."

~

A student's decision to participate in the program, undoubtedly, affects his or her parents. Parents should encourage and support their son or daughter's decision. Students' mischief is balanced with independence, responsibility, and enriching personal experiences. Not only do parents of students have bragging rights about their son or daughter working for Disney, but also they are given an excuse to visit sunny, hot Florida for a vacation.

Parents always worry about their children but some students become frustrated with their worried parents while in the program. After being in the program for two months, a student's parents continued calling her every night to make sure she was okay. The bothered student finally told her parents to leave her alone, or she would never return home. The student was true to her words as she extended for a second program and then stayed at the resort in a permanent Team Leader role. Today, she's a Guest Service Manager in Attractions.

Another student was always reminded to drive safely. After constant and annoying reminders, the student commented to his parents, "No shit! Why wouldn't I drive safe?"

The mother of a sexually-active student constantly reminded her son to wear condoms while having sex. The annoyed student should have listened to his mother because he became a very young father nine months later. He explained to his mother that condoms had nothing to do with the situation, but the magical Disney environment caused it.

The following parent testimony was obtained from www.disneyalumni.com:

A parent of a Fall, 1995 alumna remembers: "My daughter was taught dishes didn't clean on their own, a fairy didn't magically do her laundry, and green things would grow on food that wasn't put in the fridge."

A parent of a Fall, 1999 alumnus recalls: "My son learned that toilet paper must be put on the roll by a human being, sacrifices of expensive purchases must be made, oil in the car must be maintained, and bathrooms didn't clean themselves."

A parent of a Spring, 2002 alumnus remembers: "On my son's first day he called me and asked where the best place to buy toilet paper was. He learned that there would be nobody there to take care of him."

A parent of a Fall, 2004 alumnus recalls: "We visited our daughter three times during her internship. We got so caught up with the theme parks that we didn't get an opportunity to spend any time with her."

~

The presentations and interviews conclude. The internship offers are sent to students. Suitcases become packed, and checklists are slowly completed. Good-byes are made, and the time arrives to board a flight, get into a car, or catch a bus. No, this isn't a road trip. Nor is it a trip to a foreign country where studying abroad sounds appealing or Hollywood where the hope of fame and fortune exists. Instead, the destination is a place containing fantasy, wishes, dreams, and a five-foot tall rodent named Mickey Mouse.

Anticipation, excitement, fear, and curiosity become the center of emotions. What is this Disney College Program really about? What is this popular vacation destination really like? Of what will the gains consist and what losses can be expected? Once students set their feet on Walt Disney World Resort property, the real adventures begin, the memorable experiences are created, and the magical perceptions that most students have quickly change.

Chapter Two

Checking-In

Of all the things I've done, the most vital is coordinating the talents of those who work for us and pointing them toward a certain goal.
—Walt Disney

The big arrival date approaches and students begin migrating into the Walt Disney World Resort area in Lake Buena Vista, Florida. Some students arrive days before their official check-in date, while others show up just minutes prior. Students arriving prior to their start date are responsible for their own lodging. Students not driving their own automobile generally fly into Orlando International Airport. Students must arrange and pay for their own flights into the Orlando area. To most students' surprise, Disney doesn't provide airport transportation, and students must cover any expenses.

If lucky, students will arrive at the Walt Disney World Resort in a timely manner. Some students, however, find it a little more challenging. One student informed the shuttle company of his destination. Not knowing the Orlando area, the student's destination was in the driver's hands. After a forty minute ride, the student ended up at Universal Studios Orlando.

After another student's shuttle ride to an Orlando area hotel, he realized it was the wrong hotel. The lost and confused student wanted the Lake Buena Vista Days Inn and not the Orlando Days Inn.

Some students don't know the difference between the areas at which they might arrive. Such was the case with one off-course student as she trusted a taxi driver to take her to the Vista Way housing complex. Instead, she was taken to the University of Central Florida's student dormitory in Orlando. The student got out of the taxi and got in a line with other students from the university. She approached what appeared to be a check-in table and attempted to sign-in. To the lost student's surprise, she was miles away from her correct destination.

A Spring, 2005 alumna recalls: "I think it was my shuttle driver's first day because he couldn't understand English and didn't even understand the word 'Disney.' I had no idea where I'd end up. I finally told him to take me to Mickey Mouse. I was dropped off at the resort's transportation center."

~

When the big day finally arrives, students line up in lengthy lines as if it were a big E-ticket ride at one of the Walt Disney World Resort theme parks. The hot and humid morning is enough to make one sweat, but nerves and fear of the unfamiliar cause most of the perspiration. The moist air is as fresh as the students waiting in line. The lines grow larger and the chatter among students standing in line increases. The unfamiliar environment quickly grows on students and reality hits; this will be their new home for the next four to six months.

A group of happy and smiling cast members welcome students as the check-in process officially begins. After receiving nametags students are directed to a location where they receive their room assignments. After standing in more lines to be given large stacks of paperwork, students are directed to another location to take pictures for their identification card. Following the taking of pictures or mug shots, as some call them, students are sent to yet another location for more paperwork, and some are sent for medical exams such as ear or eye testing. Some students describe the process as "prison-like" and wonder why Disney personnel just don't march them into their rooms wearing shackles and orange jump suits. Other students take the opportunity to network, meet cultures from all around the world, and make new friends. While the process may seem lengthy and tedious, the time flies by quickly.

No matter how students may feel, the check-in process is organized more efficiently than one could imagine. On rare occasions, however, mistakes do occur. One patient student was in the process of getting a hearing test done as she sat in the little room with the headphones placed over her head. After twenty minutes had passed, she left the room to find out what was causing the delay. She discovered that the cast member conducting the hearing test had completely forgotten about her in the room.

Some students get caught up with the internship opportunity that they lose track of their dates. While standing in line during a spring check-in date, three students were curious as to why the line wasn't moving. After more time had passed, they realized it was the wrong line. They proceeded to get in another line, but it turned out to be a line for the Disney Animal Kingdom shuttle bus. About to give up, they asked a cast member into which line they needed to wait. To their surprise, the three students were informed that their check-in date wasn't for another four weeks.

Other students are so excited that their brains tend to malfunction periodically as one eager student experienced. The student checked-in and got into his car to drive to the location of his apartment. He backed his car out of the parking space and stopped for a moment to talk with a friend. The conversation concluded and thinking his car was still in the drive gear, the student accelerated into the car waiting behind him.

A Fall, 1997 alumna remembers: "I checked-in, received all the paperwork, and had my picture taken. Two program personnel confronted me and asked me to go with them to the office. They apologized and explained to me I was accepted into the program by mistake. After phone calls home and a great deal of shouting people, they discovered that I was indeed accepted into the program, and there was no mistake."

A Spring, 2001 alumnus recalls: "The lines were long and it was hotter than hell. Suddenly, a small riot broke out because someone cut in line. All I remember seeing was some short guy fly up against a door."

~

Depending upon the season, the check-in process is typically a two to three day process. Day One is considered to be the icebreaker for students as they're introduced to their living accommodations, surroundings, and the new world in which they're about to take part. Probably the most exciting experience for students on Day One is meeting their new roommates. Students under the age of twenty-one are placed into a wellness apartment where alcohol isn't allowed. Students over the age of twenty-one may request to live in either a wellness or a non-wellness apartment.

Students may request to share an apartment with friends; otherwise it's fair game and unknown whom or what their roommates might be. Roommates are based on arrival or departure dates, work location, gender, age, and program season.

After opening the door to her apartment for the first time, a student discovered that one of her roommates was an elementary school classmate. The two had not seen each other in over fifteen years. Even stranger, both students were cast into ticket taker roles at Disney's Animal Kingdom.

In another meeting, one student learned that his roommate was a fellow co-worker from two years back. Interestingly, the two lived three houses apart in their neighborhood but had no idea that either was participating in the program.

A Fall, 1991 alumnus recalls: "I opened the door to the three-bedroom apartment and nobody was there, or so I thought. I went to use the bathroom and this tall skinny kid dressed all in black came out, cigarette hanging out of his mouth, and a beer in one hand. He asked if I was the new guy and I was afraid to say yes."

A Spring, 1998 alumnus states: "Before you open the door to your apartment, you must have an open mind or you'll run out of there screaming. I entered the room and saw two eighteen-year-old guys on the couch kissing. They saw me and said, 'You must be the new kid.' My jaw must have reached the floor."

A Fall, 2002 alumna states: "In some cases you're assigned to a room already occupied by students. Such was my case. I put all of my things away and left with a couple of friends. I came back to the room around 1:00 A.M. and went straight to the kitchen. I turned around and standing behind me were two girls holding a baseball bat. They thought I broke into their apartment. I explained that I was the new girl, but they weren't informed of my arrival by program personnel."

A Fall, 2002 alumnus remembers: "I put all of my clothes away and left for the day without meeting any of my roommates. I came back at 2:00 A.M. and crawled into bed. A few hours later I woke up to a girl screaming her lungs off. They had put me in a female apartment by mistake. After the incident, the screaming girl and I 'hooked up' and we got married two years later."

~

Students may request to change apartment assignments, but a small fee is set in place to discourage the change. Students are known for presenting housing officials with some very creative excuses in changing assignments during their first few days.

Many students tend to use allergies as a valid excuse such as the student who wasn't happy that he didn't get assigned to the same apartment with his friend. Wanting to relocate, he claimed that he was allergic to people from the Midwest. His request was accommodated even though he was born in the Midwest.

Another student couldn't tolerate her Asian roommates' cooking, and after two days in the program, she requested to be relocated. She explained that she was allergic to Asian cuisine. The allergic student was relocated to another apartment, but her new roommates also cooked Asian cuisine. Five days after the move and still no tolerance for the smell, she quit the program.

To add to the list, a student claimed she was allergic to mold and that her apartment contained large amounts of mold. She was relocated, and, two days later, her allergies began causing her problems. Two weeks later, the concerned student visited a doctor and learned that she was indeed allergic to mold. Her original apartment contained no mold, but her new location contained mold and caused her allergy problems for about a month until she had no choice but to quit the program.

Several students use fear as an excuse, such as the student who was not pleased with living on the third floor. The student claimed to have a fear of heights and was relocated to the first floor. One week later the student complained that he was afraid of the two levels of floors above him collapsing. The student quit the program because, in reality, he just couldn't get along with any of his roommates.

Another student was assigned to a third floor apartment but claimed he had a fear of heights. Housing officials relocated the student to a first floor. One week later a housing official observed the same student standing on a third floor balcony drinking alcohol. The student didn't get terminated for lying, but he was terminated for under-aged drinking.

Annoying habits by roommates also cause the need to relocate. One annoyed student couldn't tolerate his roommate because of his constant coughing. The agitated student informed housing officials of his roommate's bothersome cough. The student was relocated to another apartment, but he had to share a room with a loud snoring student.

One frightened student requested to be relocated after his roommate experienced a nightmare. The student informed housing officials that he feared for his life and was scared that his roommate would murder him in his sleep. The student relocated to another apartment, but he quit the program two days later. No reason was provided according to a program representative.

CHECKING-IN

Sometimes honesty is the best option in requesting a change of venue. One honest student told housing officials the truth and explained that his roommates were just plain boring. He was relocated to another apartment that same day.

Another student wanted to be in the same apartment with his lover. The student informed housing officials he needed to live with his friend because he was the only one able to give him his medicine. Housing officials needed no further details or explanation and granted the request. The students were able to give each other their medicine.

A Fall, 2001 alumnus recalls: "My roommate had an odor about him that I couldn't stand. Housing officials wouldn't move me to a new location, so I said I was allergic to polyester and that his clothing was nothing but polyester. They actually fell for it."

A Spring, 2003 alumna remembers: "I wanted my own room, so I told housing officials that I had a loud snoring problem. They didn't believe me, so I pretended to snore really loud, and it drove my roommate crazy. One week later, I was relocated to another apartment, where I had my own room."

A Fall, 2008 alumna recalls: "I wanted out of my room situation, so I told housing officials that my roommates gave me nightmares and I couldn't sleep. It worked, and I was moved."

~

Day Two or Three typically involves students signing their lives away on paper as signatures are required on several important documents. Many students describe this as the most monotonous part of the entire program because they're anxious to visit the theme parks but are kept inside signing a stack of papers. During the process of signing papers, housing and program guidelines are explained. Students submit their signed paperwork, and a cheerful cast member reviews the documents for missing signatures, but some incorrect signatures do slip through every now and then.

Creative students try their best to manipulate the signature process. After turning in a stack of documents, one rebellious student was asked why he didn't sign the section pertaining to the housing guidelines. The student explained that he didn't agree with the program guidelines. After an extensive discussion with program officials, the student finally agreed and signed the documents.

Another student signed all of his documents as "Bugs Bunny." Several moments later a cast member interrupted the speaker and asked, "Will Mr. Bunny please come to the back of the room? We are missing a few signatures from him."

One clever student signed all of his documents, but he signed his first and last name incorrectly. His philosophy was that the documents would be considered invalid because the signatures were incorrect. To his surprise he had to correctly re-sign every document.

A Fall, 2002 alumnus remembers: "I just began signing papers without reading what I was agreeing to. I think this was how Disney trapped us."

A Spring, 2003 alumnus recalls: "I just started signing my name as 'Mickey Mouse.' Program personnel never called me on it, so I doubt if they even checked."

A Spring, 2004 alumnus remembers: "I signed my name as 'Michael Eisner,' the CEO of Disney. A day later I was asked to return to the housing office. Program personnel asked me to re-sign all of my papers because, to their knowledge, Michael Eisner was not in the College Program."

A Fall, 2005 alumna states: "Lawyers or cops probably don't have to sign that many papers. It really felt like Disney took all of our rights away, and, if we did one thing wrong, it would be all over."

~

After the first few days in the program, students familiarize themselves with the Walt Disney World Resort, the housing complex where they reside, and the Orlando area. The first week moves at such a rapid pace that some students go days without sleeping. A new lifestyle presents itself to students, and they're eager to take advantage of everything possible.

A majority of students become so tired that their bodies finally give up, causing them to fall asleep in some odd places. After not sleeping for two straight days, one student fell asleep in his car while waiting at a red light. Five minutes had passed, and the student woke up to a police officer knocking at his window.

Another student fell asleep on the Vista Way shuttle bus after her first evening of work. The exhausted student made seven trips to the Magic Kingdom and home before she was awakened by the bus driver.

Sleep is generally not a priority for most students, as one student's belief was, "I'll sleep when I'm dead." During a three day period, that brave student visited every Disney theme park, three local beaches, seven Orlando area nightclubs, and drove to Key West. The following six days she overslept and was late to work each day. She was terminated from the program but had the opportunity of taking in many sights before her early departure. Apparently, she didn't understand the meaning of pacing oneself.

A Spring, 2000 alumnus remembers: "There wasn't enough time in the day to do everything, and sleep was the last thing on my mind. I slept on the bus rides to work. I also fell asleep in the shower several times. One night I slept for two hours in the shower, got out, and went to a party."

A Fall, 2003 alumna recalls: "I didn't sleep at all during my first three days. On my first day of work, I overslept and was two hours late."

A Spring, 2004 student remembers: "I fell asleep during my first day of work because I didn't sleep during the first few days after I arrived in Florida. My trainer sent me home so I could catch up on my sleep. I went home, crawled into bed, and five minutes later my friend called me. I went to Daytona Beach instead of sleeping."

~

There are students who don't last the first few days of the program and mysteriously disappear. Some quit the program within days of checking-in because of either long-distance relationships not working out, homesickness, or failure of adjusting to the new environment.

Not being able to withstand a long-distance relationship, one student decided to quit the program after two days because she missed her boyfriend. She packed her bags and flew home, only to discover that her boyfriend was accepted into the program. He was going to surprise her the day after she left, but it backfired on him. The boyfriend remained in the program, and the two lovers ended their relationship one week later.

In a separate incident, an eighteen year old female student couldn't tolerate being away from her thirty-five year old boyfriend. The student quit the program, went home, and caught her boyfriend cheating on her with an even younger girl.

Students who can't make it through the homesickness generally quit the program without informing their roommates or program personnel. An unusual student unpacked her suitcases, packed the cupboard with groceries, and purchased a small television. Three hours later she repacked her suitcases and mysteriously quit the program. Her roommates were grateful to get the free groceries and the television for their living room.

One student unpacked his suitcases, greeted his roommates, and then repacked his suitcases. One hour later he quit the program but left a friendly note on the kitchen counter that stated, "Thanks for the good times, short and sweet."

Adjusting to the Florida environment can be difficult for some students to overcome. One student couldn't adjust to the extreme humidity and believed it would ruin her clothing. She came to the conclusion that it would be cheaper for her to move back home.

In a rather bizarre incident, one female student quit the program because she claimed two male students propositioned her to participate in a threesome on her third day. Instead of reporting the incident, the female student just decided to quit the program. No charges were filed, and her claim wasn't validated by program officials.

Adjusting to the Disney environment can be equally difficult for some students. After three weeks into the program, a rather odd student couldn't handle the daily Disney mindset. She didn't want to quit the program but believed termination was a better option. While looking through her roommates' personal items, she was caught by two of her roommates. A report was made, and one day later the troubled student instigated a fight with another roommate. Her wish was finally granted as she was terminated from the program. For this peculiar individual, her dream did come true. As the disturbed student turned in her housing ID, she asked, "So, why'd I get terminated?"

A Spring, 2000 alumna remembers: "One hour after my roommate moved in, she moved out. I didn't understand why she left so quickly after being in the program for just one hour. Two weeks later I learned from a friend that she was offered a management position with Universal Studios Orlando."

A Fall, 2002 alumnus recalls: "Our roommate mysteriously left the program on his third day without telling anyone. We assumed he was just homesick. We later found out that his parents had won the state lottery."

A Spring, 2003 alumnus remembers: "There were six of us in the apartment, and my five roommates were assigned to work at It's a Small World. On my fifth day, I came home from work and all five of my roommates had quit the program and checked-out. I had the entire apartment to myself for the following week until two more students were assigned to my apartment. Surprisingly, the two students worked at It's a Small World, too. Three days later both students quit the program and checked-out. I had the entire apartment to myself for another two weeks, and it was party central."

~

Students begin settling into their new environment and learn about the people with whom they'll spend the next few months living. Their clothes are put away, the kitchen becomes stocked with food, and the program guidelines are set in place. The "new" quickly wears off for students as they learn the magic isn't what they had hoped for and the pay isn't worth their troubles. The homesickness begins settling in, and the excitement phase quickly passes. For the students who don't bail out to go home, they make the best of the institutionalized situation and have the greatest time of their lives.

Chapter Three

Mouse-Washed

Part of the Disney success is our ability to create a believable world of dreams that appeals to all age groups. The kind of entertainment we create is meant to appeal to every member of the family.
—Walt Disney

Wasting no time and before students can take a breather, they're sent off to the Disney University where they participate in *Traditions*. This unique training process is a company-wide orientation program which educates newly recruited cast members about the company's history. Cast members play trivia games, interact with fellow cast members, and listen to top Disney executives talk to them via a recorded video feed. Cast members also listen to a recorded video feed from the company's Chief Executive Officer which attempts to convince them how exciting and honorable it'll be to work in a magical kingdom. After the video feeds are presented, the official Mouse-Washing begins.

"To all who come to this happy place – Welcome. Disneyland is your land. Here age relives fond memories of the past and here youth may savor the challenge and promise of the future. Disneyland is dedicated to the ideals, dreams and the hard facts that have created America, with the hope that it will be a source of joy and inspiration to all the world."

When Walter Elias Disney dedicated Disneyland on July 17, 1955, the world was introduced to its first theme park. The magical place dedicated to the ideals and dreams that created America would quickly catch on with the public. The success of Disneyland was endless, but the land wasn't. When building Disneyland, Walt bought only enough land upon which to build his park on. Hotels, restaurants, and other private entities quickly began construction around Disneyland, crowding in on Walt's fantasy world. In hindsight, Walt wished he had purchased enough land to include all of the extra amenities to make his magical land complete and self-sustaining.

During the early 1960's, Walt and his team began scouting potential locations around the United States for his next theme park. After an extensive search that included locations such as St. Louis and the Great Smokey Mountains, Central Florida became the location of choice. If word got out that Walt was in search of property, the cost of land would have dramatically increased. Walt's team of executives purchased the land under aliases, preventing real estate prices to escalate. One of the aliases used was Retlaw Enterprises, which is Walter spelled backwards. When Walt visited the Central Florida location, he would keep out of sight. On most occasions, Walt flew over the location via helicopter so he would not be discovered.

Walt purchased over twenty-seven thousand acres, about forty-three square miles. The swamp property was twice the size of Manhattan Island and the same size as San Francisco. The average price per acre was around $180, with the final cost a little over $5 million. Walt could finally create a fantasy world large enough to keep the realities of the real world away from his magical kingdom.

On November 15, 1965, Walt held a press conference in Orlando where he revealed plans for a vacation retreat which included theme parks, resort hotels, golf courses, and his city-of-the-future. He also announced that over seven thousand acres would be permanently kept in their natural state. Today, close to nine thousand acres are kept in their natural state. Days after Walt's announcement, the cost per acre increased to $80,000.

Sadly, Walt Disney would never see his Disney World project turn into a reality. On the morning of December 15, 1966, the world lost its greatest dreamer. Walt Disney passed away due to complications from lung cancer. The Central Florida theme park project looked bleak, but Walt's brother Roy was determined to see the project through.

Roy O. Disney changed the project name from Disney World to Walt Disney World, so the entire world could remember Walt and everything in which he believed and for what he stood. The project was so extensive that the company decided to build the resort in phases. Construction began in April, 1969, and took a little over two years to turn Walt's vision into a reality.

On October 1, 1971, the Magic Kingdom opened its gates as Roy O. Disney dedicated Walt Disney World:

"Walt Disney World is a tribute to the philosophy and life of Walter Elias Disney...and to the talents, the dedication, and the loyalty of the entire Disney organization that made Walt Disney's dream come true. May Walt Disney World bring Joy and Inspiration and New Knowledge to all who come to this happy place...a Magic Kingdom where the young at heart of all ages can laugh, and play, and learn - together."

Walt Disney World opened with Magic Kingdom Park, Disney's Polynesian Resort, Disney's Contemporary Resort, and Disney's Fort Wilderness & Campground. Immediate success followed, and the company's sights on expansion were imminent. Roy Disney retired immediately after Walt Disney World's opening, and two months later he passed away.

Today, Magic Kingdom Park contains over fifty attractions in six themed lands including Main Street U.S.A., Adventureland, Frontierland, Fantasyland, Liberty Square, and Tomorrowland. The outdated Mickey's Toontown Fair is no longer as the park moves forward with its updated Fantasyland project. Classic attractions include Space Mountain, Big Thunder Mountain Railroad, Splash Mountain, Pirates of the Caribbean, Haunted Mansion, It's a Small World, Jungle Cruise, and Peter Pan's Flight.

Magic Kingdom Park was built with a foundation below its surface containing a nine-acre tunnel system, also known as the utilidors, providing warehouses, storage areas, hallways and offices. Unknown to most guests, Magic Kingdom Park is actually the second floor. The multi-functioning basement is the nerve center for the park's highly sophisticated computer systems. Playback recordings in each attraction, fireworks, and parade operations are all controlled beneath Magic Kingdom Park.

An Automated Vacuum Assisted Collection (AVAC), the first waste system of its type installed in the United States, is linked through the utilidors by pneumatic tubes. Trash is deposited in several collection points around the park. Every fifteen minutes the trash is drawn through the tubes at speeds of up to sixty miles per hour and sent to a central compactor station. The utilidors allow Magic Kingdom Park to function efficiently and unnoticeably to park guests.

In 1975, The Walt Disney Company announced plans to build Walt Disney's ultimate dream. The Experimental Prototype Community of Tomorrow (Epcot) was announced with slight modifications to Walt's original plan. Walt wanted a working and living community home to over twenty thousand residents which would create and test new technologies and inventions of tomorrow. Community buildings, schools, businesses and homes were to be built in a circle. Business and commercial areas would be at its center while community buildings, schools, and recreational complexes would be around it with residential communities along the perimeter. Sophisticated People Movers and monorails would provide efficient transportation while automobile traffic would be kept underground.

Walt Disney stated: "It will be a planned, controlled community, a showcase for American industry and research, schools, cultural and educational opportunities. In EPCOT there will be no slum areas because we won't let them develop. There will be no landowners and therefore no voting control. People will rent houses instead of buying them, and at modest rentals. There will be no retirees; everyone must be employed."

Instead of an actual working city of the future, Epcot would be a showcase of ideas, a place for people to come and learn about themselves and the world around them, through the use of Disney technology and entertainment. The theme park would be a very different experience than the Magic Kingdom. Known as the largest construction project in the country at the time, Epcot began taking shape in 1979 with over ten thousand workers involved.

Epcot's landmark, Spaceship Earth, took a little over two years to build and became the world's first geodesic sphere. One hundred eighty feet in height, the sphere is actually composed of two spheres, one inside the other. The inner sphere contains the track and rooms of the attraction. The outer sphere is held about two-feet away from the inner sphere by aluminum hubs.

On October 1, 1982, exactly eleven years after Magic Kingdom Park opened, Epcot opened its gates to the world. With Walt Disney's wife Lillian present Card Walker, then Chairman and Chief Executive Officer of Walt Disney Productions, dedicated Epcot:

"To all who come to this Place of Joy, Hope and Friendship, Welcome. EPCOT is inspired by Walt Disney's creative vision. Here, human achievements are celebrated through imagination, wonders of enterprise and concepts of a future that promises new and exciting benefits for all. May EPCOT Center entertain, inform and inspire and, above all, may it instill a new sense of belief and pride in man's ability to shape a world that offers hope to people everywhere."

Today, Epcot is divided into two sections, Future World and World Showcase. Future World consists of a variety of experiences that explore innovative aspects and applications of technology from some of the world's greatest inventors. Future World is home to such attractions as Innoventions, Soarin',

Mission: SPACE, and Test Track. World Showcase is made up of eleven pavilions that celebrate cultures from around the world: Mexico, Norway, China, Germany, Italy, United States of America, Japan, Morocco, France, United Kingdom, and Canada.

After the opening of Epcot, The Walt Disney Company experienced some dark days as corporate takeovers and buyouts seemed all but a reality until Roy E. Disney, Walt Disney's nephew, recruited Michael Eisner. As the company's new Chief Executive Officer, Eisner guided the company's growth and continued the expansion of the Walt Disney World Resort. Eisner and company executives wanted resort guests to stay on Disney property and spend more money during extended stays. With that said, construction began on the resort's third theme park and a handful of resort hotels.

In 1988, the first luxury resort, Disney's Grand Floridian Beach Resort, opened on the shores of the Seven Seas Lagoon and across from the entrance to Magic Kingdom Park. The appealing red and white Victorian architecture lures its guests into a first-class resort. Many of Disney's Fairy Tale Weddings take place on-site, and the elegant location provides a breathtaking backdrop. The first moderately priced resort, Disney's Caribbean Beach Resort, opened to resort guests. The five brightly colored island villages provide a tropical environment for resort guests. Epcot continued entertaining guests from around the world, and the company introduced Illuminations, an epic show containing pyrotechnics, spotlights, special effects projectors, and themed music.

In early 1989, the Walt Disney World Resort's third major theme park was nearing completion. Disney-MGM Studios would be the new home of thrilling movie themed attractions and the Walt Disney Animation Florida division. A replica of

Grauman's Chinese Theater, the world's most famous and recognizable Hollywood movie house, was constructed as the park's icon. On May 1, 1989, Michael Eisner dedicated the park:

"The world you have entered was created by The Walt Disney Company and is dedicated to Hollywood--not a place on a map, but a state of mind that exists wherever people dream and wonder and imagine, a place where illusion and reality are fused by technological magic. We welcome you to a Hollywood that never was--and always will be."

Disney-MGM Studios was an instant success, and future park expansion plans were immediately put into action. In 1994, an entirely new street known as Sunset Boulevard opened and became home to the one hundred ninety-nine-foot tall Twilight Zone Tower of Terror, the tallest attraction on property. Other attractions include George Lucas' Star Tours, Jim Henson's Muppet Vision 3D, The Great Movie Ride, Rock 'n' Roller Coaster, Toy Story Midway Mania, Fantasmic, and the Indiana Jones Epic Stunt Spectacular. In 2007, the theme park's name was re-branded to Disney's Hollywood Studios.

Pleasure Island, an elaborate nighttime entertainment complex, also opened in May, 1989. Pleasure Island was an area of themed nightclubs within the Downtown Disney District. According to Walt Disney Imagineering's fictional back-story *(Disney Legend)*, the island's nightclubs were once home to a shipping company owned by the adventurous businessman Merri-Weather Pleasure. A great storm destroyed the business, and Mr. Pleasure disappeared, but the warehouses remained behind. Known as the hotspot for students and cast members, the clubs closed its doors in September, 2008. For many program alumni, this was seen as a sad day.

A Fall, 2006 alumna states: "We'd go for free every Monday night. We'd leave at 6:00 P.M. and wouldn't get home until 4:00 A.M. am. Back at work at 6:00 A.M. So many memories. It's a shame Disney closed it."

A spring 2007 alumnus asks: "Now where do the CPs go? Nothing else could ever compete with Pleasure Island. That was our place every Monday and Thursday nights."

In June, 1989, Typhoon Lagoon opened to the public. The resort's second water park (River Country was the resort's first and closed in 2001) contains ships, fishing gear, and surfboards that are strewn about after, according to *Disney Legend*, a typhoon struck. The centerpiece of the park is "Miss Tilly," a shrimp boat impaled upon a "volcanic peak" that erupts water every half hour.

The Walt Disney World Swan and Walt Disney World Dolphin opened in 1990. Neither owned nor operated by The Walt Disney Company, the eye-catching architecture features oversized geometric buildings and windows and five-story tall statues of swans and dolphins on the rooftops. Disney's Yacht and Beach Club Resorts also opened in 1990. The two hotels share similar themes and are connected together by a common recreation area, health club, and restaurant. The unique swimming area between them is called Stormalong Bay and features a sand-bottom lagoon. A one hundred fifty-foot tall water slide originating from a shipwreck on the beach makes for a daring adventure for those brave enough for the challenge.

Disney's Port Orleans Resort opened in 1991, and Disney's Dixie Landings Resort opened in 1992. The backwoods' theme combined with atmosphere of the French Quarter and New Orleans, makes the resort a quaint destination for guests.

Disney's All-Star Sports and Music Resorts, surrounded by larger-than-life icons familiar with each genre, opened in 1994 followed by the opening of the Wilderness Lodge Resort Hotel.

Blizzard Beach, the largest water park at the Walt Disney World Resort, opened in 1995. According to *Disney Legend,* an unexpected snowstorm blew through the area, leading to the construction of Florida's first ski resort. Naturally, the snow didn't last long and melted, leaving behind a collection of waterlogged ski jumps and chair lifts. The failed resort was in the process of closing for good when an alligator was seen sliding down a flume and splashing into a pool of water. The ski resort was reborn as a water park, with the alligator as the park's mascot.

Disney's Wide World of Sports opened its doors in 1997. The sports complex contains a main event stadium; a multi-sports field house for basketball, volleyball, and gymnastics; a tennis arena, baseball diamonds, soccer fields, outdoor tracks, weight rooms, racquetball courts, classrooms, and broadcast facilities. From high school, college and youth team levels, to amateur and individual professional athletes, sporting events from all fields take place in the state-of-the-art facility. In addition to the sporting complex, the Walt Disney World Resort includes five world-class golf courses and two themed miniature golf courses: Fantasia Gardens and Winter Summerland.

On April 22, 1998, the Walt Disney World Resort's fourth major theme park opened its gates. Disney's Animal Kingdom would be a tribute to the animal world and conservation. The five hundred acre theme park contains exotic habitats from around the world. The park also features imaginative attractions, celebrating animals of today, the mythical, and the extinct. Michael Eisner dedicated the park on opening day:

"Welcome to a kingdom of animals...real, ancient and imagined: a kingdom ruled by lions, dinosaurs and dragons; a kingdom of balance, harmony and survival; a kingdom we enter to share in the wonder, gaze at the beauty, thrill at the drama, and learn."

Divided into six themed lands, the park celebrates Asia, Africa, DinoLand U.S.A, Rafiki's Planet Watch, Camp Minnie-Mickey and Discovery Island. The park's icon, the Tree of Life, is fourteen-stories tall and was sculpted by more than one dozen artisans. The swirling tapestry of three hundred twenty-five animal carvings creates a staggering spectacle that can only be fully appreciated by seeing the landmark in-person.

Attractions include Kilimanjaro Safaris, Kali River Rapids, Dinosaur, and Festival of the Lion King, which is one of the resort's highest rated attractions by its guests. In 2006, the park welcomed its newest attraction Expedition Everest, a high-altitude and high-speed train adventure sending guests backwards into a terrifying encounter with the mysterious Yeti.

~

According to a March 30, 2004, article from the *Orlando Sentinel*, five thousand cast members are dedicated to maintenance and engineering, including over six hundred horticulturists and six hundred painters. The Walt Disney Company spends more than $100 million every year on maintenance at Magic Kingdom Park. The streets in the theme parks are steam cleaned nightly. A tree farm is located on property so that when a mature tree needs to be replaced, a thirty year old tree will be available to replace it. There is a fleet of Disney operated buses on property which is free for use by resort and park guests. Taxi boats link some locations. A fleet of eleven monorails also operates at the Walt Disney World Resort linking Magic Kingdom Park, Epcot, the Contemporary, Polynesian, and Grand Floridian resorts, and Ticket and Transportation Center (TTC). An express monorail connecting the TTC and Magic Kingdom Park is also available. The Walt Disney World Resort's monorail system is perhaps the most well-known monorail system in North America. When not in operation, the monorails are housed in the resort's "Roundhouse" located behind Magic Kingdom Park. Today, the Walt Disney World Resort covers a total of forty-seven square miles, and only one-quarter of the property has been developed.

Even though the back-stories of how the Walt Disney World Resort came to fruition excite some students, there are those who don't experience that same passion. One student booed Michael Eisner when he spoke to the group via a recorded video feed. The disrespectful student explained that he booed Eisner because he had no respect for him and his beliefs.

During one class a trainer began talking about how great his trip to Disneyland Paris was. A student asked, "What does this have to do with us and Walt Disney World?" The sidetracked trainer resumed his discussion about the Walt Disney World Resort.

One male student was so infatuated with one of the female trainers that he asked her out on a date. The trainer explained that she was married and the student asked, "So, will you still go out with me?" The student never did get a date with the trainer.

A Spring, 2002 alumna recalls: "During a video discussing the magical moments of the Disney environment, I was so joyful and excited that I needed to leave the room because of excessive tears."

A Fall, 2004 alumna remembers: "Disney Mouse-Washed us into thinking the place and even the program was bigger than it really was."

A Spring, 2005 alumnus recalls: "Orientation was long and boring. In every class there always has to be a 'kiss-ass' who makes it even longer with his or her irrelevant comments!"

~

After the *Mouse-Washing* concludes, a second type of orientation occurs which is more specific to one's work location such as the Magic Kingdom, Epcot, resort hotels or other areas. Students get an understanding of the area in which they'll be working, and at the end of the orientation day, if not done so already, are informed of the role into which they've been cast. Two or three days into the program, a student's excitement can turn sour if he or she is cast into an undesired role.

Most students are cast into a role without even knowing what the role will be until either their arrival date or second orientation date. Various roles are available across the entire resort. The most common roles into which students are cast are Operations, Quick Service Food and Beverage, Full Service Food and Beverage, Merchandise, Lifeguard, and Custodial. Students may request preferences of roles and even locations, but there are no guarantees. There are certain roles students desire and some roles they literally fear.

Students hope for roles where they'll be working in the outdoors, the water, and the warm Florida sunshine and not in roles relating to either food or garbage. The consensus among students is that Operations is the most desired area to work. Most want to work in Operations, which include theme park attractions such as the Jungle Cruise, The Great Movie Ride, Haunted Mansion, or Space Mountain. Students fear attractions such as It's a Small World due to that infamous song repeated over-and-over, or the Tomorrowland Indy Speedway because of the fumes from the little gas-operated cars. Operations also include Parking and Park Greeter roles.

A Lifeguard role at one of the water parks or resort pools is the second most popular role in which to be cast. Warm sun, tanning, half naked guests, and blue water aren't bad ways to spend four to six months. Some students prefer the indoor air-conditioned environment of Merchandise, while others don't mind making the streets sparkle in a Custodial role under the warm sun. Other roles for which students might be considered are Hospitality, Character Attendant, Transportation, Resort Hopper, Costuming, PhotoPass Photographer, and Character Performer.

Students not cast into their desired role attempt to find clever ways of getting out of what potentially could be a long four to six month sentence. Not all excuses work on managers at the Walt Disney World Resort as there are some managers who are smarter than the average mouse. One student claimed he couldn't work in Quick Service Food & Beverage because he was allergic to fast food. This claim came two hours after his trainer saw him eat a hamburger and fries. The student wasn't transferred to another role.

After being assigned to work as a Vacation Planner, a student claimed she couldn't sit for long periods of time because of a rare butt disease. She was cast to work in Operations but claimed she couldn't stand for long periods of time. When asked what role the student preferred, she suggested Lifeguard but warned that she had a fear of water. The student eventually quit the program after she wasn't transferred to a Lifeguard role.

In a reasonable excuse, one student was assigned to work in Parking, but he claimed having a fear of getting hit by moving automobiles and would be traumatized by any type of accident. The student wasn't transferred, and two months into the program he was struck by an automobile. He wasn't badly injured and remained in the role for the duration of the program.

Some students' excuses are so far out in left field that they should be relocated just for their creative efforts. One student didn't want to work at The Many Adventures of Winnie the Pooh because she claimed to have a fear of bears and owls. She was transferred out of Fantasyland and moved to Tomorrowland attractions.

Another student refused to work at The Many Adventures of Winnie the Pooh because he couldn't tolerate Christopher Robin. Management asked the student why he couldn't tolerate Christopher Robin and the student said, "He's a weenie! Put me at an attraction where there are tough characters." The lucky student was transferred to It's a Small World.

One student refused to work at Muppet Vision 3D because of nightmares of the puppets that she had as a little girl. After two weeks of making her claim, she was transferred to another attraction.

In yet another odd excuse, a student didn't want to work at It's a Small World because he claimed to have a fear of singing dolls. The student got stuck with the singing dolls for six months. He decided to return for a summer program the following year, and out of all of the attractions possible, he was assigned to It's a Small World for three months. No word yet on whether his professional internship will be as a Guest Service Manager for It's a Small World.

An International student was cast to work at the Hall of Presidents but refused to work at the attraction because he believed President George W. Bush was a murderer. He was relocated to another attraction.

A rather unusual student indicated that he couldn't work at Space Mountain because the last time he went into Space he got lost. Perplexed at this comment, management asked where he'd prefer to go. The student stated, "Under the sea." He wasn't transferred and remained in space for four months.

Before students provide their creative excuses, they should be knowledgeable about their requests. One confused student didn't want to work at Peter Pan's Flight but requested to work at the Batman ride. Management explained that the Walt Disney World Resort didn't have a Batman ride, but the student didn't believe them and quit the program.

Another clueless student didn't want to work at the Magic Kingdom and asked to be transferred to Sea World. The disappointed student learned that Sea World wasn't a Walt Disney World Resort property and quit the program.

A rather bold student was assigned to work in a Character Attendant role but wanted to work in Attractions. Upset with his role, the student began informing young guests that the characters weren't real, and there were people inside the costumes. Not to the student's surprise, he wasn't around shortly thereafter.

A Fall, 1988 alumnus remembers: "Disney put me in one of the Main Street U.S.A. shops, the Emporium I believe. I didn't travel clear across the country to work in a store. I told the trainer I couldn't work in a store because I had a fear of being robbed. The trainer just laughed at me. One week later, a guest stole a Mickey Mouse doll, and I tried the excuse again with my manager. He actually believed the excuse and transferred me to attractions."

A Spring, 1995 alumnus recalls: "I got cast to work at It's a Small World and didn't even want to consider working at that attraction. I explained to my trainer that I had a fear of water and a fear of falling in and they bought it!"

A Fall, 1996 alumnus states: "If you don't like where you're working, make some realistic story up and Disney will move you to a different location. I was placed at Epcot's Spaceship Earth to work, but that is one of the slowest paced attractions at the entire resort. The ride has a lot of mechanical functions and continuously moves, like the Haunted Mansion. I could have worked at the attraction, but wanted to be outside with all of the girls, so I told them I had a fear of loud machinery and heavy equipment. They moved me outside to Parking."

A Spring, 1998 alumna recalls: "I was cast to work at Splash Mountain and told them I had a fear of steep drops. My manager told me I wouldn't have to ride the attraction, but I explained that just looking at the drops gave me nightmares."

A Spring, 2001 alumnus remembers: "I was cast as a Custodial Host, but I wasn't going to spend my hot summer days cleaning up people's crap. I told my trainer I was allergic to shit. He looked at me and said, 'Tough shit!' "

A Spring, 2006 alumna states: "During cast members' first week of training, they're required to wear a little red badge that states, 'Earning My Ears.' This little slogan indicates to everyone that you're a rookie, don't know what you're doing and are at the bottom of the seniority food chain."

MOUSE-WASHED

A Fall, 2009 alumnus recalls: "I told them the truth. I said I didn't want to work around kids. My manager clarified to make sure I knew kids were part of the role. I said yes, but I said kids drive me nuts. My manager said, 'I know. Let me see what I can do.' I was placed backstage in costuming."

~

When Magic Kingdom Park opened in 1971, the Walt Disney World Resort employed a little over five thousand cast members. Today, the resort employs close to sixty thousand cast members and is the largest single site employer in the United States. As students quickly learn, the demand to fill positions is quite high. After resources are exhausted in and around the Orlando area, the company has a desperate need to fill a high amount of empty positions on the front lines. Students come to the realization that they're the bodies that help fill the continuous need of staffing at the Walt Disney World Resort. Do students succeed? Does students' work ethic pay off for the company? Even more importantly, do students respect the Disney magic?

Chapter Four

Earning

You reach a point where you don't work for money.
—Walt Disney

The pixie dust wears off, and students must quickly learn how to whistle while they work. Low pay and long hours give students serious doubts as to why they signed up for the College Program in the first place. As of 2010, the hourly pay rate was $7.25-$8.39 depending upon the assigned role. Six day work weeks are typically required during the peak seasons, and it's common to work fifty to sixty hours per week. Some students may work over seventy hours per week, with overtime rates applied.

Superior guest service tactics and Fortune 500 company philosophies are enforced. Responsibility in the workplace is quickly tested, and opportunities to learn about intercultural interactions exist. The balance of one's work life and personal life are practiced. Students must battle with the daily pressures of the Disney mindset and strive forward in whichever role they might fill at the Walt Disney World Resort.

The College Program calls the Walt Disney World Resort the student's *Learning Laboratory*. There are several other forms of terminology used in the College Program which students learn about within their first few days of work. Historically, The Walt Disney Company has implemented the use of *Disney Speak*. A customer is referred to as a *Guest*, and an employee is recognized as a *Cast Member* since he or she is cast into a *Role* and not a position. Cast members wear *Costumes* and not uniforms. A crowd is referred to as an *Audience*. A ride is called an *Attraction* or an *Adventure*. A ride operator is called an *Attraction Host/Hostess*. At work or in the park is called *Onstage* and behind the scenes away from guests is called *Backstage*. Security guards are called *Security Hosts/Hostesses* and janitors are referred to as *Custodial Hosts/Hostesses* as they clean up a guest's *Protein Spill*, which is *Disney Speak,* but in reality it's nothing but vomit. An ambulance is referred to as an *Alpha-Unit*. Also of noteworthiness is that during the first forty or so years of Disney theme park operations, managers or supervisors were referred to as *Leads*. Recent changes now have *Leads* referred to as *Guest Service Managers (GSM)* and *Coordinators*.

Throughout the years of the College Program's existence, most students have created their own Disney terminology, the College Program terminology. Every student knows at least one or more of what most refer to as *CP Lingo*. College Program Cast Members are referred to as *CP, CPer, Closing Person, Company Pee-On, Constantly Poor, College Puke*, or *Corporate Prisoner*, just to name a few.

A Fall, 2003 alumnus best describes the company and College Program terminology as the following: "As a CP we're cast into a host or hostess role that takes place onstage or backstage of an attraction or adventure where we serve guests until we're either extended or early released by some power hungry GSM or are carted offstage by an alpha-unit."

~

All Disney cast members are expected to follow a dress code or as the company calls it, *The Disney Look*. Students must maintain good stage presence by demonstrating professionalism and good judgment at all times in regard to their appearance. No matter where students work or of what their role consists, attitude and performance are direct reflections on the quality of the Disney show.

Chewing gum, smoking, and drinking are all prohibited while onstage, but there are always students who create their own rules. After one student finished chewing her gum while onstage, she spit it out into an empty stroller, or so she thought. A young girl was asleep in the stroller as the used gum landed on her face. The guilty student quickly vacated the area and pretended nothing ever happened.

One student entered an onstage area holding a lit cigarette. As the student walked past a cast member holding a bouquet of balloons, she popped two balloons with her cigarette. The student's manager observed the entire incident from a distance and suspended the student. The student never returned.

Another student mistakenly walked onstage while smoking a cigarette. A manager confronted the student and took him backstage. The student feared being reprimanded, but the manager asked if he could borrow a cigarette. The two had a smoke offstage together and discussed what time they'd be heading to Pleasure Island that evening.

During one afternoon an intoxicated student didn't care about the Disney experience and walked onstage while drinking from a bottle of beer. A Security Host escorted the under-aged drinker backstage, and the student was terminated from the program.

Sleeping, moodiness and eating are all prohibited while onstage. One student working at the Twilight Zone Tower of Terror fell asleep while leaning up against a wall. For twenty minutes, guests were confused as to whether the student was a real person or a robot. The student received a verbal warning.

In one incident a guest asked a frowning student why she wasn't smiling. The bothered student stated that she "didn't get any" the night before. It's unclear if that student was smiling the following day.

Then there's the starving student who pulled out a sandwich and began eating while loading guests into boats at the Pirates of the Caribbean. A guest asked where he could purchase a similar sandwich, and the student responded, "My apartment." The guest reported the student to the attraction's Team Leader, and the student received a verbal warning.

A Fall, 2000 alumnus recalls: "I was hungry during a shift and a guest holding a bucket of popcorn wasn't looking, so I grabbed a handful."

A Spring, 2001 alumnus remembers: "I badly needed a cigarette and was all out, so I asked a guest if he could spare one. I let him and his family move to the front of the line at Space Mountain in exchange for a cigarette."

A Spring, 2003 alumnus recalls: "A bunch of us wanted to call and check the scores of a basketball game. I'd go off into a corner and make the calls. The last time I went to the corner my manager was standing there waiting for me. I got yelled at by him even though he was always on his personal cell phone."

~

Disney is a first-name organization, and every cast member in the company is referred to by his or her first name. Even top executives and park management are on a first name relationship with every Disney cast member. All cast members are issued a nametag which must be worn at all times while onstage. Cast members are permitted to have their hometown city and state or country engraved on their nametag.

Students may choose to have the name of their college or university in lieu of their hometown. One student had "University of Michigan" engraved across her nametag. A guest asked the student where Michigan was located and she replied, "Michigan." The guest accused her of getting smart with him and reported her to a manager.

Another student had his nametag engraved with his hometown of Los Angeles. A guest approached the student and informed him that was where all of the bad people lived. The student ignored the guest and continued with his daily duties.

Even though nametags are required, one student refused to meet the requirement in his own subtle way. After not wearing his nametag for two months, the student was reprimanded for not following company policy. He asked management why they didn't reprimand him two months earlier, and management explained that they gave him the opportunity to get it right. The confused student contacted the Human Resources department about the situation, and when it was all said and done, management was also reprimanded for their lack of actions as the student continued working in the program.

A Fall, 2000 alumna remembers: "I lost twenty-two nametags while in the program. Two months after I returned home, I found five of my nametags being sold on Ebay."

A Spring, 2003 alumnus recalls: "My nametag said I went to the University of California at Los Angeles. A guest told me he went to UCLA and that it was a much better school."

~

Students are expected to work nights, weekends, and holidays during the College Program. Students are guaranteed to be scheduled a minimum number of hours but will most likely work over forty hours per week. The College Program used to have a cap on the number of hours students are scheduled, but that policy and mentality seems to be thrown out the door due to staffing needs. The Walt Disney World Resort is always looking for extra bodies to fill shifts. It's common to walk into a break-room and see several exhausted students who are worn down and half asleep from working so many hours.

Students have the option of working more hours if they choose and are compensated for any overtime accumulated. One student worked over one hundred hours during a one-week period. When asked by fellow cast members why he was working so many hours, the student explained that he wanted to see how long it would take before he collapsed to the ground. The student didn't collapse but did earn a rather large paycheck.

A Fall, 2001 alumna recalls: "Disney worked all of the CP's every opportunity they got. I worked four fifteen hour shifts in five days."

A Spring, 2003 alumna remembers: "Nobody was in our break-room, so I fell asleep on the couch in there. Three minutes later, I woke up and two other CP's were next to me sleeping. It was tiring for everyone at times but a lot of fun."

~

No matter into what role students are cast, rude and demanding guests do cause problems, fellow cast members create havoc, and the Disney experience can lose its magic. Whichever might occur, many students are involved in some interesting situations, and they attempt to handle them with the best of their newly trained Disney abilities.

Students cast into Operations are placed into one of three roles: Attractions, Parking, or Park Greeter. Responsibilities include loading and unloading guests, operating sophisticated ride systems, memorizing and delivering lengthy narrations to large groups, staffing Toll Plaza areas, cash handling, operating a motorized vehicle, operating turnstile areas, light cleaning, and assisting with audience control.

After park hours one fall evening, two students jumped into the Jungle Cruise's river and swam around the attraction in a race. When the two swimmers arrived at the finish line, their manager was waiting on the loading dock to congratulate them on their accomplishments. Needless to say, that was their last night in the program. Perhaps the two students should have requested to work in a Lifeguard role.

Working in attractions requires cast members to conduct ride-throughs to make sure the show elements don't have any malfunctions. During one student's ride-through of the Haunted Mansion, the sleepy student took a nap. His fellow cast members left him alone, and it wasn't until after eight passes through the attraction that he woke up from his nap to a friendly greeting from his manager. The student wasn't terminated but did have a nice long conversation with his manager.

Three students decided to get out in the show scenes of Pirates of the Caribbean with the pirates themselves. As boats full of guests slowly passed through a scene, the students would run up to the water and attempt to scare the guests. The three students were caught when a guest complained that the pirates in the ride were malfunctioning because they weren't scaring anyone. The students weren't terminated from the program, and they never did a stunt like that again or at least while on-the-clock.

When attractions close for unexpected repairs, cast members are required to inform guests of the closures by respecting the magic. For example, cast members can inform guests that the pirates are sleeping or the bears are eating. No matter of what the excuse might consist, the magic can never be broken. Some students like to spice up the magic. During a one-hour closure of The Many Adventures of Winnie the Pooh, a guest asked when the attraction would reopen. The student explained that the attraction would continue operation after Tigger sobered up from his drinking party with the Disney princesses.

A creative student stood in front of the Haunted Mansion during a two-hour closure and explained to passing guests that the mansion was no longer haunted. The guests believed the student and would tell other guests that the mansion was no longer haunted.

After closing Pirates of the Caribbean for the remainder of the day, a student explained to guests that the pirates went to Key West for the day and wouldn't be returning until the following morning. The pirates did return, and the attraction re-opened the following day.

After one student was asked why the Magic Kingdom closed at 7:00 P.M., he explained it was a special evening where the employees wouldn't have to tolerate stupid guests. The guest said, "That sounds fun."

While walking past the ice cream parlor on Main Street U.S.A. one afternoon, two guests and a student saw a rat run across the sidewalk. The student informed the guests, "Don't worry, that was just Mickey's cousin." It's unclear if the cousin ever found its way back to Fantasyland.

Even though an attraction may be fully operational, many students continue creating magic for gullible guests. As one student loaded guests into the boats at Pirates of the Caribbean, a little girl asked him if the pirates were mean. The student responded, "They'll only be mean to your mommy and daddy." Pulling at her parents' hands, the little girl screamed and begged for them not to go on the attraction.

In another creative act of magic, a group of students placed a Chucky doll in It's a Small World. Terrified children in boats wondered why the evil doll was attacking another doll in the attraction. Even though the doll wasn't really attacking any other doll, a parent complained to one of the students working at the attraction. The student explained, "Sometimes the dolls turn evil." The doll was immediately removed by the students.

One guest asked why It's a Small World didn't feature any Irish dolls. The student explained that it was because the canal water would have to be replaced with Guinness. The guest remained confused as she got into the boat.

A group of guests asked how much it would cost to spend the night in the Twilight Zone Tower of Terror. The student explained that it was a ride and not a hotel. The guests wouldn't take no for an answer, so the student said the cost would be $50. The four guests each gave the student $50, and they were directed to see the bellhop inside the attraction. After complaining to management, the student returned the money to the guests and later got terminated for the scam.

One student decided to create his own magic. During a performance of the Magic Kingdom's Spectromagic, the student was scheduled to work Parade Audience Control. After management couldn't locate the student in his assigned area, they discovered him sitting on the curb and watching the parade while eating ice cream. The student was given a verbal warning but was later terminated for repeating the same action.

A Fall, 2003 alumna recalls: "I worked as a Park Greeter at the Magic Kingdom. I got the opportunity to watch the fireworks from the roof of the Emporium."

A Spring, 2004 alumnus remembers: "I was moving tables and chairs from an area on Main Street U.S.A. while working Parade Audience Control. The tables were heavy, and I dropped one on my toe. I screamed, 'Shit.' A little girl pulled at her mother's shirt and said, 'Mommy, mommy, that man said the shit word.' I hid for a few moments, so I wouldn't get in trouble. To my knowledge, no complaint was ever filed."

A Fall, 2007 alumnus recalls: "I was working at Mickey's Philharmagic and a guest asked if the ride was fast. I said it was a show. They asked if the show was fast. I said it was a fast-paced show. They asked to complain to a manager because they believed Fantasyland shouldn't have any fast-paced rides."

A Spring, 2009 alumna remembers: "I worked as a host at Expedition Everest. A guest asked if Disney would reimburse their vacation if they didn't see the Yeti. I said that there was a disclaimer on the back of each ticket regarding attractions. They said 'We got free tickets; would that disclaimer still be on the back?"

~

Students working in Parking and the Parking Toll Plazas at the theme parks can be exposed to the wild Florida climate during their shifts. Managing automobiles, guests, and the weather can create several obstacles.

Providing guests with misleading information is common, and the guest reactions provide other magical moments. During one opening hour, a guest drove up to the Magic Kingdom Toll Plaza and asked if it was the correct place to park for the Magic Kingdom. The student redirected the guest to park at Disney's Hollywood Studios, at the time Disney-MGM Studios, and said, "Special people like you are allowed to park over there." The guest said, "Yes, you're right. I am special." The guest turned around and drove away from the Magic Kingdom.

Another guest asked why Disney charged for parking. The student explained that it was because the CEO of Disney, at the time Michael Eisner, needed more money. The guest backed up his automobile, burned rubber, and drove away from the Toll Plaza.

Other students attempt to bargain with motorists for the cost of parking. One student was so thirsty that when a guest drove up to his Toll Plaza, he exchanged free parking for a half bottle of water. The student learned his lesson and ensured he'd always have water nearby.

Another student was so hungry that when a guest drove up to her Toll Plaza, she exchanged free parking for a McDonald's Big Mac. Not stopping there, she exchanged her cast member jacket for some fries and gave away her cast member hat for a small soda. At the conclusion of her program, she received a bill in the mail for her lost jacket and hat. She never paid the bill.

Students are notorious for mischievous behavior during their shifts. During one slow afternoon, a group of students started a game of cone bowling in the parking lot. After setting the cones up for one of the rounds, a nearby motorist sped up and wiped out the cones. The guest yelled out the window, "Strike!"

One student was so bored working at the Magic Kingdom parking lot that one day he brought his pair of roller blades with him to work. During the middle of the afternoon, he strapped his roller blades on and skated throughout the lot. After five minutes of skating, the bored student was rushed to a nearby hospital as he crashed into a parked automobile. His injuries were minor compared to the major verbal warning he received from management.

A Spring, 2003 alumnus remembers: "I worked in the Toll Plaza booth one afternoon and fell asleep for about ten minutes. I woke up to a car honking at me. I looked closer at the vehicle and noticed it was one of my managers visiting the park on his day off."

A Fall, 2005 alumnus recalls: "Working in Parking, we'd see the guests early in the morning when they were happy. If we worked the late shift, some guests would be happy, sad or screaming mad. One night, a father was so upset with his experience that he demanded I give him his money back, even if it had to come out of my own pocket. I explained that I couldn't help him, and he demanded I turn my wallet over to him. I called security just in case."

A Spring, 2006 alumnus remembers: "A mother sitting on the back of the Magic Kingdom parking lot tram yelled at me about how her day was miserable. I said, 'Hey lady, go to Epcot tomorrow and bug them!' The lady told me she'd indeed go there and not give Disney any money ever again. I guess she didn't realize that Epcot was still a Disney theme park."

~

Quick Service Food and Beverage cast members are responsible for taking meal orders, operating a point-of-sale system (cash register), cash handling, filling food orders, dispensing and selling alcohol, heavy lifting, pushing and pulling, emptying waste cans, general cleaning with chemicals, and food preparation.

Working with food can provide students with several opportunities of creating "other" types of magic for guests and fellow cast members. One student was extremely bored during a shift and decided to write notes on a few cups, wrappers, and napkins. He wrote, "For a good time, visit Vista Way" and left his phone number. While at home that night, the lucky student received a phone call, however; the caller was none other than his manager from work. The student didn't return to work the next day.

During a guest service interaction, a rather large guest complained that his hamburger was prepared incorrectly even though he'd already eaten the entire hamburger. The student said, "From the looks of it, you don't need another hamburger." The complaint was filed with Guest Relations but no action was taken against the student.

One clumsy student dropped a basket full of popcorn onto the ground. Instead of sweeping the popcorn into a dustpan, the student placed the popcorn into a large popcorn bucket. The bucket was given to his manager as a special gift. It's unknown whether the manager ate the gift.

A Spring, 2004 alumnus recalls: "I was serving alcohol at Epcot and couldn't take it anymore, so I took a drink while onstage. Before I was finished, I had put away seven beers."

A Fall, 2005 alumna states: "CP's assigned to work at the resort other than Food and Beverage shouldn't complain. Working with food can be hot, monotonous and demanding. It's perfect for those pursuing a career in culinary but not anyone else."

A Spring, 2006 alumna remembers: "I loved working in Food and Beverage because I never went hungry. We were fed a lot of times and when we weren't, we'd feed ourselves from the food supply."

~

Merchandise cast members are responsible for operating a point-of-sale system, cash handling, stocking shelves, preparation of food/candy, package delivery, stroller rental, heavy lifting, pushing and pulling, light cleaning, selling of alcohol and tobacco, and providing information to guests.

Disney calls their Merchandise division, *Merchantainment*. Students working in *Merchantainment* interact with guests who are eager to spend hundreds of dollars in a matter of seconds. Students only need seconds to create their own entertainment. A confused guest asked a student working in the Main Street U.S.A. Emporium where she could meet Bugs Bunny and Porky Pig. The student explained that those characters weren't affiliated with Disney. The upset guest requested to speak with a manager, so the student informed the guest that she could meet Bugs Bunny and Porky Pig at Mickey Mouse's house in Toontown.

In a potentially dangerous incident, a guest returned her stroller to the Magic Kingdom Stroller Shop but forgot to take her baby. A student went to stack the stroller, only to realize a screaming baby was left behind. The stroller baby and mother were quickly reunited.

In another stroller incident, a guest asked if she could rent a stroller to haul her personal items around the park. The student informed her that she couldn't and suggested that she and her husband go make a baby. The guest asked, "What happens next?" The student just walked away from the confused guest.

Another guest asked a student working at an outdoor merchandise cart in Disney's Animal Kingdom if they would turn the air-conditioner on for the outside. The student explained that the air-conditioner would kill the animals.

Disney's Walk Around the World is a way for families to leave a lasting memory at the Walt Disney World Resort. Guests may purchase a brick and get their names engraved on that brick. The brick is placed into the ground at the front of the Magic Kingdom's main entrance. One guest asked what the purpose of purchasing a brick was. The student explained that it was a cheap way for Disney to repave the walkways.

Epcot offers a similar memory called *Disney's Leave a Legacy*. Families may leave a picture of themselves, which is engraved into a concrete shaped tombstone located beyond Epcot's main entrance. The area looks like a miniature concrete cemetery. One guest asked what the cement blocks symbolized. The student explained that all of the people who die on Walt Disney World Resort property are buried there. The female guest turned to her husband and said, "Baby, we should die here at Disney World."

A Fall, 2002 alumnus recalls: "A guest left his cell phone behind in the store, so I put it in a drawer. After a couple of rings, I answered the phone and it was the guest. He told me he'd be right back to pick up the phone. The phone rang again, and I looked at the caller ID, which said 'Evil Fat Ass.' When the guest came in to get his cell phone, he said his girlfriend had been trying to call him. I was curious and asked who 'Evil Fat Ass' was, and he said, 'Oh, that's my grandmother.' "

A Spring, 2003 alumna remembers: "I was working in the World of Disney Store when a guest asked where the bathrooms were located. I gave him directions, but as I walked through the store five minutes later I noticed a guest had left their 'human waste' in the middle of the floor. I called my manager but he didn't believe me. A guest approached and informed me that someone had 'gone to the bathroom' around the corner. A second person had used our floor as their bathroom. As I dialed the phone to contact my manager, I heard a guy in the distance cursing. I looked over and saw that it was my manager as he just stepped in the 'human waste.' I approached him and asked, 'Do you believe me now?' "

A Spring, 2005 alumnus recalls: "While working at Epcot, a guest asked where the nearest Wal-Mart was located. I wanted to smack the lady, but I informed her that the nearest Wal-Mart was located in the round white ball (Spaceship Earth). Her eyes lit up."

Another Spring, 2005 alumnus remembers: "A female guest asked where Wally-World was located. First, I explained that it's called Wal-Mart and not Wally-World. Second, I informed her that we didn't have a Wal-Mart on Disney property. The lady said, 'But there's a McDonald's on-site.' I finally gave up and informed her that a Wal-Mart was located in Disney's Animal Kingdom, near the crocodile pit. She thanked me and went on her way."

A Fall, 2005 alumna states: "Working in Merchandise allows most CP's to work in an air-conditioned building. During one afternoon at Disney's Animal Kingdom, a guest asked if he could stay in the building until it cooled off outside. I explained that he was in Florida, and it rarely cooled off. The upset guest told his wife they should've gone to the Magic Kingdom instead."

~

PhotoPass photographers assist guests with photo memories. These are the cast members asking, "Can I take your photo?" They'll either be working in the streets in front of a Disney landmark, with a character, or in a highly populated area with guests. Guests provide each photographer their PhotoPass card, and the pictures can be downloaded from the Internet if the guest chooses to do so.

Students have to stand for long hours and battle the hot Florida sun in this role, and one student decided to help the time fly by a little quicker one afternoon. The student began taking photos of random women walking by. Management quickly learned what was occurring and approached the student. When asked what his reasoning was for doing such a thing, he stated, "I needed better shots than the families I've been shooting." The student would have to shoot photos back home because he quit the program that afternoon.

A Fall, 2009 alumna states: "Working as a PhotoPass Photographer is a good role because it has high levels of interaction with guests, you can move around a little, and there's some freedom away from management."

A Fall, 2009 alumnus remembers: "I was always asked to take pictures of people with their own cameras. They would say 'Hey, ask the camera guy.' Sometimes I'd snap photos of people and cut their heads or bodies off in the picture, so when they got home they'd have a nice surprise. The problem I ran into was that most people liked to immediately check their photos on the camera. I'd play dumb and just apologize. One guest actually asked, 'How'd you get your camera license with crappy shots like this?'"

~

Lifeguards are responsible for monitoring the safety of guests as they swim, providing limited emergency medical attention, keeping pool areas clean, and providing guest information. In addition to keeping the pool areas safe, there are students who try to do a little more. During one warm afternoon, a large guest wearing a two-piece bathing suit walked past a student. Without thinking, the student yelled, "Put some clothes on!" The guest turned around and slapped the student across the face. The guest didn't report the comment to management but the student learned his lesson.

In a separate guest encounter, a male guest asked if Typhoon Lagoon had a Titanic ride. The student pointed to a rather large woman sitting at a nearby table and said, "Yes, we do; she's right over there." To the student's surprise, the large woman was the wife of none other than the male guest.

Injuries do occur often, but one student discovered that getting immediate emergency assistance can be complicated. The unlucky student was walking to his work location at Typhoon Lagoon for the start of his shift when he suddenly slipped and fell. He broke his ankle and could barely get to a phone to call for help. He tried calling his manager for assistance but had no luck. After yelling for help, he decided to call for an *alpha-unit* which came to assist fifteen minutes later, or so he claims. He was rushed to a nearby hospital and released later in the day. The student returned to work the same day, in crutches, and was asked by his manager why he wasn't working. To the student's surprise, not one cast member or manager knew what had happened. The manager wasn't concerned about the student's injury but only when he could return to work. The manager asked, "Can you work anyways?" The student didn't return to work that day and took three days off to recover.

A Fall, 2004 alumnus recalls: "I loved working as a Lifeguard because it was a buffet of beautiful women. If an ugly woman came up to me and asked if I worked there, I'd just say my shift was over. If they were cute, I had all day."

A Spring, 2005 alumna remembers: "As a Lifeguard you get to work on your tan while enjoying the warm sun. A guest came up to me one day and asked how I got such a nice tan. I hesitated for a moment and said, 'Um, I'm a lifeguard and I'm out here every day.' The guest asked me again. I finally told her that Disney provided us with magical tanning location."

~

Custodial cast members are responsible for emptying waste cans, cleaning restrooms, bussing tables, sweeping and mopping, working with cleaning chemicals, vacuuming, dusting, cleaning pool decks, and providing guest information. Students in the Custodial role have the honor of making the magical resort shine and creating an opening day environment. Some students like to create other environments as well. One student working at Epcot was carrying his dustpan when a guest alerted him that his pan was on fire, most likely from a lit cigarette. The student panicked and tossed his pan into the World Showcase lagoon.

During one afternoon, two students decided to conduct a sword fight with their brooms while onstage. Before a manager could confront the two, a broom went flying into the air and landed in a nearby stroller that was occupied by a young infant. The two students were given a warning.

In a separate incident, a guest standing next to a trashcan asked where the nearest trashcan was located. The student pointed to the one he stood next to, but the guest tossed his trash on the ground and said, "Pick it up yourself!" Some guests will never learn.

A Spring, 2001 alumnus states: "Working in Custodial gives you a little more freedom to roam around the park. Even though you're assigned to an area, a lot of custodians venture out and mess around. I was assigned to work at Main Street U.S.A. in the Magic Kingdom. I actually went to watch Illuminations at Epcot during my shift one evening. While watching Illuminations, a guest asked if I worked there. I said, 'I don't work here, I work at the Magic Kingdom, which reminds me, I need to get back over there.' I returned to the Magic Kingdom and nobody ever knew what I did."

A Spring, 2003 alumna states: "Only at Disney does a computer tell you when you can use the bathroom. Working in Custodial gives you the freedom to use the bathrooms whenever needed. I was cleaning the bathrooms one day and had to 'go' really bad, so I just used the stall I was cleaning."

A Fall, 2004 alumnus recalls: "As I carried my dustpan and broom in the Magic Kingdom, a guest asked if I worked there. I told her that I always carried a dustpan and broom with me while on vacation."

~

Vacation Planner cast members are responsible for selling Walt Disney World Resort ticket media, learning computer-based ticketing systems, assisting guests with itinerary planning, and providing them with information. Some guests request additional assistance from Vacation Planners as one student experienced. A guest asked why he had to pay for admission into Epcot. The student explained it was the policy, but the guest said he and his family should be let into the parks for free because they paid taxes. After the student explained the admission policy, the guest said, "Well, I think you should pay our way in!" Needless to say, the student refused to pay their way in and the guest provided payment for entry.

A Fall, 2003 alumna states: "Selling tickets also means taking families' money. A guest complained to me that admission prices were too high. I explained that he didn't have to pay and could take his family elsewhere. The guest said, 'Four tickets please.' I guess my point wasn't taken."

A Spring, 2005 alumna states: "You get to sit in a chair for most of the time while working as a Vacation Planner. I remember getting up to push the tickets through the window slot and when I sat back down, the chair busted. I fell flat on my ass and got back up. The next guest in line saw what had happened, but he just asked if I was okay enough to sell him his tickets."

~

Transportation cast members are responsible for staffing the resort Monorail and/or watercraft. Driving vehicles, delivering narrations during trips, loading and unloading guests, and assisting with audience control are all associated with the Transportation role. Students have the opportunity of becoming either the first or last point of contact for guests visiting the resort. One guest asked if the monorail would take him and his family back to the airport. The student explained that the monorail wouldn't, but the family believed they came from the airport via the Walt Disney World Resort monorail. The student asked the family to quickly board the monorail, but the family changed their mind and the father said, "Wait, a boat brought us here from the airport." It's unknown whether that family ever made it back to the airport.

Another guest was about to board the monorail from the Magic Kingdom station when he claimed to have parked his car at the Magic Kingdom and didn't take a monorail to the front gates. The student explained that he most likely parked his car in either the Magic Kingdom or Epcot parking lot. The guest refused to board the monorail. The student said, "Sir, see that large lagoon of water? Your car is parked on the lagoon. Feel free to help yourself." The guest thanked the student and quickly proceeded down the Monorail exit ramp and toward the lagoon.

One attractive guest asked where her off-property hotel was located and how she'd find her way back. The student commented, "I don't know, but can I come with you for maybe some sex?" The student's request wasn't granted, but management was quick to grant him a quick trip home for his comment. It turned out that there were additional complaints about the student regarding similar comments.

A Spring, 2004 alumna recalls: "A guest asked if he and his family could sit in the front of the monorail with the driver. I told them they had to be of Royal descent in order to be allowed up there."

A Fall, 2005 alumnus states: "It's fun to work with watercraft at the resort. My costume clearly looked like a sailor's outfit. A guest asked if she could speak with someone who worked on the boat. I said I worked on the boat but the guest didn't believe me. I finally told the guest that she could find people who worked on the boat over at the monorail."

~

Hospitality cast members are responsible for checking guests in and out of resorts, processing payments, assisting guests with itinerary planning and ticket sales, tagging and delivering luggage, answering guest phone calls, and providing information to guests. Finding other tasks to accomplish while in the role are common as was the case for two adventurous students. During a slow afternoon, the two students decided to take a Port Orleans Resort Hotel golf cart out for a joy ride. Normally, the golf cart is used for transporting guests and luggage to their rooms. As the driver approached a small lake, he lost control and slammed into the shallow end. As the two students quickly attempted to push the golf cart out of the water, their manager arrived. Both students were suspended.

In a separate incident at the All-Star Music Resort, one student was so bored during his shift that he borrowed a golf cart. After a few moments of joyriding, the journey concluded when the student slammed the golf cart into the resort's swimming pool. The student argued that it was an accident and only a verbal warning was issued.

A Fall, 2003 alumnus recalls: "While taking a guest's luggage to his car, I commented that his luggage was really heavy. The guest told me it was because of all the towels he stole from his room. He tipped me $50 and I never said a thing."

A Spring, 2005 alumnus states: "You learn a lot about people while working in Hospitality. While working at the front desk, an older couple asked where we sold sex toys in the hotel. Terrified, I informed them that the Magic Kingdom sold all the sex toys that are available at the resort."

~

Character Attendant cast members are responsible for directing guests while taking appropriate photographs with characters, providing audience control, setting up and removing stanchions, ropes and poles, retrieving and arranging strollers, and maintaining cleanliness and order of a work location. Two students decided not to maintain the order of their work location as they began playing around with ropes before sectioning off Main Street U.S.A before an upcoming parade. A competitive game of tug of war broke out and one student let go of the rope, sending the other student into the lap of a guest sitting on the curb. More significantly was that a group of top-level Disney executives were within seconds of approaching the infamous *CP* tug of war.

Character Attendants are also responsible for maintaining show quality and character integrity, but some students like adding a little flavor to some characters' personalities. After asked where Donald Duck was located, a student explained, "You can find Donald over at Minnie's house but don't tell Mickey."

In a separate incident, a guest asked if Mickey Mouse would be coming back out later in the day. The student explained that Mickey Mouse wouldn't be coming out later because he would be getting wasted at Donald Duck's party.

Another guest asked where Donald Duck's house was located. The student explained, "Mr. Duck's house was destroyed by last week's hurricane." A young girl in the group began crying and the student said, "Don't worry sweetie, Mickey's house was destroyed, too."

One guest asked where Mickey Mouse's yacht was located. The student explained that Mickey didn't have a yacht, but the guest wouldn't accept no for an answer. Giving up, the student informed the guest that Mickey's yacht was located in Daytona Beach.

As one student escorted Minnie Mouse offstage, a guest asked why Minnie didn't come out with Mickey Mouse. The student explained, "Mickey and Minnie are currently going through a tragic divorce."

A student working as Ariel's Character Attendant was asked if Ariel's breasts were real. The student said, "Yes, they are, feel them when you get up there." To the student's surprise, the guest approached Ariel and grabbed her breasts.

Working as a Character Attendant requires interacting with many types of parents. While escorting Chip and Dale offstage, a student was knocked to the ground by two parents who wanted their three children to meet the two chipmunks. The injured student got up and shoved the parents into the direction of three Security Hosts. The family was escorted out of the park.

In a separate incident, the cast member playing Mickey Mouse mistakenly autographed a young boy's book as Minnie Mouse. The mother of the boy asked the Character Attendant why Mickey signed the book as Minnie. The student explained Mickey Mouse was a transvestite. The upset mother reported the student, and he was suspended for the inappropriate comment. The student was on previous warnings for similar comments to both guests and cast members.

A Spring, 2002 alumnus recalls: "As I escorted a worn down and exhausted Goofy offstage, an angry father confronted me and demanded that Goofy stay longer to meet his kids. I stopped and asked the father if he'd rather have Goofy pass out backstage or out in front of his kids and have them see Goofy carted off by the paramedics. The father said, 'Just as long as my kids get to see Goofy, I could care less if he dies on the stretcher! Now, let my kids see him!' I refused the request and continued escorting Goofy backstage."

A Fall, 2005 alumna states: "As Character Attendants we're essentially the bodyguards for characters. As I escorted Mickey Mouse offstage one afternoon, an angry mother grabbed Mickey's arm. Before I could do anything, a group of kids began attacking the mother because she was hurting Mickey. The mother started pushing the kids and before I knew it, I was breaking up a fight between a forty year old mother and a group of twelve-year-old kids."

A Fall, 2009 alumnus recalls: "I was escorting Mickey Mouse when I heard a dad tell his kids, 'There's Mickey Mouse, go kick him!' The kids began running toward us, and I had to run interference."

~

The Zoo is located in the Magic Kingdom utilidors and is where the entire Magic Kingdom cast of characters meet up for costuming, breaks, and other related functions. This central location is a great place to damage all of the Disney magic that has been in place for over decades. Students working at the Magic Kingdom get to experience firsthand what the Zoo is all about because they have to pass through to reach their work locations. Here, Snow White may have a cigarette hanging from her mouth, Peter Pan might be cussing, Mickey Mouse may be dropping 'the F word' all over the place, Goofy could be making a drug deal with Donald, and Prince Charming might be kissing Hercules.

Character Performer cast members bring Disney's famous character personalities to life. The role is in a fast-paced and physically demanding environment working in hot, confining costumes. On some days, however, the student performers let their costumes get the best of them. One student dressed as Goofy had a protein spill while inside his costume and onstage. He couldn't get offstage for another ten minutes.

In a separate incident, a student dressed as Pluto had a protein spill while inside his costume and onstage. As he walked offstage, a young boy asked why he was leaving. Going against the rules of not speaking while inside his costume, the student said, "Mickey Mouse gave me a poisoned dog bone."

While playing Cinderella, a student asked a young boy with whom he was at the park. The five year old boy said, "My daddy and his secretary but it's a secret from my mommy."

In another odd incident, a forty year old male guest asked the student playing Snow White out on a date. Taken aback, the student explained that she was already dating five of the seven dwarfs. The guest yelled to his friend standing to the side, "Hey, Snow White's a slut!" The friend asked the student playing Snow White if she could fit him into her busy schedule and she replied, "Sure, after Sneezy!"

A Fall, 2002 alumnus remembers: "I was in the Tigger costume and a young boy kicked me in the rear. I kicked him back until he fell to the ground screaming for his parents. After several kicks, my Character Attendant quickly escorted me offstage before the parents could catch me. I was suspended and was lucky for not being terminated."

A Spring, 2003 alumnus recalls: "I was in the Pluto costume and a cute mother asked me to sign her son's autograph book, so I signed it with just my phone number. Five minutes later, a guy came up to me and shoved the autograph book in my face. He informed me that he was the lady's husband. Before things escalated, I quickly ran offstage."

A Fall, 2004 alumna states: "Most of the cast playing characters are gay. During my program, I remember the guy who played the Queen of Hearts was dating the guy who played Goofy."

~

Holidays at the theme parks bring in large crowds, which cause extended hours of operation. Holidays also require most students to work on these special days. Whether it's Easter, Fourth of July, Halloween, Thanksgiving, Christmas or New Year's Eve, students unite with fellow cast members to celebrate the holidays while working their long shifts.

During one Valentine's Day visit to the park, a guest asked if the Walt Disney World Resort would be doing anything special for the romantic occasion. The student informed the guest that Mickey and Minnie Mouse would be "getting it on" later in the evening. A child in the group asked, "Can we come, too?"

During one Easter week holiday, a young guest asked if the Easter Bunny would be making an appearance at the Magic Kingdom. The student explained that the Easter Bunny wouldn't be coming because he and Mickey Mouse didn't get along with each other.

As the Fourth of July approached, a guest asked if there would be fireworks on that day. The student explained that The Walt Disney Company didn't celebrate Independence Day and no fireworks would take place. The fireworks did go off that evening, but it's unclear whether the guest stayed around for the show.

As the Headless Horseman rode his horse down Main Street U.S.A. during *Mickey's Not So Scary Halloween Party*, a mother asked why the guy had no head. The shocked student responded, "We caught him stealing, so we cut his head off and made him ride down the street in shame." The mother's seven year old son began crying and said, "Mommy stole something from the store. I don't want her to die!"

Thanksgiving, Christmas, and New Year's are the busiest times of the year for the Walt Disney World Resort. The increased attendance can cause some very chaotic days, and most students try working through the special occasions with the highest spirits. On the day before Thanksgiving, a guest asked if the Magic Kingdom would be serving turkey for the special day of giving thanks. The student informed the curious guest that once Mickey Mouse killed the bird, dinner would be served.

During one Christmas season, a mother asked a student working at the Magic Kingdom's *Mickey's Very Merry Christmas Party* why it was snowing in Florida. The student explained it was fake snow, but the flakes were deadly if consumed. At that moment, the mother's daughter ran up and said, "Mommy, Mommy, I caught the snow on my tongue." The mother panicked and demanded to see a doctor.

Moments after a New Year's Eve celebration began, a guest asked what the big celebration was all about. The shocked student explained, "Uh, we're celebrating the closing of Walt Disney World. After tonight, they're tearing this place down." The guest said, "Oh, I'm glad we came today."

In Fall, 1999, a student working on New Year's Eve was asked if the Walt Disney World Resort was prepared for Y2K.

The student explained that the park would explode at the stroke of midnight. The park has yet to explode.

Some holidays give students the opportunity to celebrate in their own magical way. During one Easter holiday, a student colored Easter eggs for the occasion but colored the eggs unlike any others had been colored before. The student colored and labeled all of the eggs with a College Program theme. Some eggs consisted of the College Program logo, program phrases, and various X-rated materials. There was even a Vista Way egg.

During a *Mickey's Not So Scary Halloween Party*, three students ate twenty bags of candy between them in one evening. Before the party concluded, their manager caught the students backstage and forced them to finish off the last bag as their punishment. The students were sick for the following three days.

A Fall, 2003 alumna recalls: "The Headless Horseman would ride his horse down the street for the Halloween parties. The horse knew the parade route and the cast member riding the horse had to have a lot of trust in the horse. One night, the horse turned a tight corner and knocked a guy to the ground. He was okay but we all laughed really hard. Five minutes prior to the accident, we politely asked that guy to move from that location as it was unsafe. The guy cursed at us, told us to 'screw off' and said that he could do anything he wanted. Justice was served on that night."

A Fall, 2005 alumna remembers: "A guest asked if we could set the Main Street U.S.A. Christmas tree on fire because he wanted to see what a burning tree looked like. I suggested that he set his own Christmas tree on fire and he said, 'But my house would catch on fire.' I asked a Security Host to keep a close eye on the tree for the remainder of the evening."

~

Park closures are rare for the Walt Disney World Resort but they do occur from time-to-time. The Walt Disney Company made history by closing all four theme parks for the first time during Hurricane Floyd in 1999 but the hurricane ended up missing the area. Hurricanes Charley and Frances came through the area in summer, 2004, and the parks were closed for each. Many students were assigned to the hurricane ride-out crews, where long and tiring shifts took place while they catered to resort guests.

During the Fall, 2004 ride-out of Hurricane Charley, a guest asked if the Walt Disney World Resort had a hurricane ride. In disbelief, the student responded, "No, but if you step outside you can experience the real thing."

Another guest asked if warm hurricanes created snow. The shocked student explained, "At least four-feet of snow but only inside the Magic Kingdom."

In a separate incident, a student worked a few hours of a ride-out at one of the resort hotels but decided to finish the remainder of his shift on a barstool at the hotel's bar. After one hour of drinking, his manager approached the bar and said, "Smart move, I think I'll join you."

During another ride-out in 2004, a student's mother called and asked how the weather was. The student answered, "Um, a boat's missing, half of a deck is wiped out, and I think a light pole just flew past my window. Other than that, it's nice and warm."

A Fall, 2004 alumna remembers: "Working the ride-out crew was like one big slumber party. Most CP's took the time to socialize while getting paid a lot of overtime."

A Fall, 2004 alumnus recalls: "I worked with about ten part-time cast members and I brainwashed them into the 'CP way.' After the hurricanes passed, all ten of those cast members came to Vista Way and partied on a regular basis."

Another Fall, 2004 alumnus remembers: "When one of the hurricanes was passing through, I went outside to take a look, and all I remember seeing was mouse ears fly past me. It symbolized the entire catastrophe."

~

On September 11, 2001, the United States of America experienced one of the darkest days in its history. Immediately after the terrorist attacks, the theme parks were evacuated and closed as the world attempted to understand where this dark day would be heading. Cast members and park guests cooperated together as the theme parks were evacuated. The following announcement was made at Magic Kingdom Park:

"Due to circumstances beyond our control, the Magic Kingdom is now closed. Please follow the direction of the nearest Cast Member."

The theme parks reopened the following day but to a different world and to a different environment. During the days and even months that followed, security was tightened and attendance dropped. For most students and cast members, the toughest part of the entire experience was trying to stay happy. Cast members and students continued creating magical moments for every guest who visited the Walt Disney World Resort. The following testimony was obtained from students working on that tragic day.

A Fall, 2001 alumnus remembers: "It wasn't a happy time and every time we heard what sounded like a plane, we held our breath."

A Fall, 2001 alumna recalls: "I honestly thought Walt Disney World was going to be a target after the Twin Towers got hit."

A Fall, 2001 alumna remembers: "I learned a lot during my program, but it wasn't until after 9/11 that I learned there were just some things more important than college parties or being a minute late for work."

Another Fall, 2001 alumna recalls: "A guest asked if Disney had a ride based on the terrorist attacks. I explained that Disney didn't have such an attraction. The guest requested to make a suggestion. Even in times like 9/11, the idiots always come out."

~

Celebrities frequently visit the Walt Disney World Resort, and students routinely have the pleasure of meeting a select few of the popular personalities. Whether the interaction is brief or extended, students enjoy meeting those whom they admire and even those whom they can't tolerate.

In one memorable celebrity encounter, an honored student was asked to escort a young unknown band before and after their performance at Pleasure Island. The student didn't recognize the group nor understand their name, but according to him they were one of the nicest groups of artists with whom he had interacted. The evening concluded, and he learned the group was none other than *Selena and Los Dinos*. The performance took place weeks before Selena was murdered. According to other cast members and students, Selena had a warm and caring heart toward everyone with whom she interacted during that memorable evening.

Many professional sport figures visit the Walt Disney World Resort each year. As one student walked past former San Francisco 49'ers' quarterback Steve Young, the brave student shouted, "Joe Montana is much better than you!"

Another student had the opportunity to meet former NFL player and broadcaster O.J. Simpson and was even invited to have dinner with him. The student refused the offer. Not quite sure why he'd refuse such an offer.

In another celebrity interaction, a student was approached by professional skateboarder Tony Hawk and was asked if he could get some extra Mickey Mouse stickers. The student gave Hawk a roll of stickers, and Hawk asked for two more rolls. Were the Mickey Mouse stickers used for Tony Hawk's skateboards?

During a visit by professional golfer Tiger Woods, a student shook Tiger's hand and said, "Mr. Woods, congratulations on winning the Stanley Cup. You're my favorite basketball player." Someone should have informed the bewildered student that Tiger Woods played golf, and the Stanley Cup was part of the National Hockey League.

Entertainers come across students, and magical moments occur quite often, or at least most of the moments are magical. While walking through the Magic Kingdom utilidors, one student got the opportunity to meet pop singer Brittany Spears. Shocked at the opportunity, the male student asked, "Are you dating anyone?" Spears smiled, "You're cute, kid, but no thanks."

During a taping of *The Wayne Brady Show*, former Walt Disney World Resort cast member Wayne Brady had lunch with a couple of students. When the students' manager learned about their lunch with the celebrity, he confronted the students and explained they were not allowed to talk with celebrities. One of the students said, "Wayne Brady invited us, if you have a problem, go talk to him!"

While backstage one fall afternoon, a student walked past singer Raven Symone and sarcastically commented under his breath, "Girl's got some shoes!" Raven smiled and said, "Thanks, I like them, too."

During one celebrity encounter, *Lord of the Dance's* Michael Flatley asked a student where the men's restroom was located, while looking directly at the restroom sign. After Flatley exited the restroom, he asked the student, "So, you work here?" The student sarcastically explained that he did work there and would not be wearing a ridiculous costume for no reason whatsoever.

A Spring, 1996 alumnus recalls: "George Foreman was a co-host on the Disney Channel's 'Inside Out.' After filming an episode, he and a few cast members from the show asked me to join them for lunch. Foreman was extremely nice and a down-to-earth guy. We must have talked for at least two hours after lunch. Foreman filmed another episode a few days later and he asked me out to lunch again."

A Fall, 1998 alumna remembers: "During my program I got to meet Robin Williams, Billy Crystal, Ben Stiller, Michael Eisner, Jennifer Lopez, Tom Hanks, James Woods and President Bill Clinton. Nobody needed to go to Hollywood because Hollywood always came to the Walt Disney World Resort."

~

College Program students and cast members work together side-by-side at their work locations. A certain level of friction does take place between the two. Cast members see College Program students as a group of cheap labor eating away at their hours and as a waste of space. Most cast members don't give students the time of day.

A Fall, 2003 alumnus states: "We can co-exist, but cast members look at us as if we're just there to party and not work. We aren't given a chance the minute we walk through the door."

A Fall, 2004 alumna recalls: "A cast member kept accusing me of taking long breaks. One day I notified our manager that I believed it was the complete opposite. As it turned out, the cast member was taking the long breaks and she was the one to get reprimanded."

A Spring, 2005 alumna remembers: "I was being harassed by a couple of cast members. It wasn't sexual harassment, but harassment in one form or another. My manager wouldn't do anything about it because I was leaving three weeks later. I went to Human Resources and they investigated the situation. My manager was talked to for not taking my complaint seriously. A few days later, other cast members were harassing me about being a 'snitch' and I just couldn't take it anymore, so I quit the program. A few weeks after I quit, I learned that those cast members were terminated."

~

Magical moments often occur between students and guests. These are the moments which make the Walt Disney World Resort a magical destination for visitors. Students create magical moments that put a smile on a young child's face or a sparkle in a parent's eye that is taken home for a lifetime.

While walking past a family prior to the Magic Kingdom afternoon parade, a student noticed a young boy crying while sitting on a park bench with his parents. The curious student approached the family and asked if everything was okay. The mother explained that her son wanted an autograph from Peter Pan, but they were leaving for the airport in fifteen minutes. The student quickly went backstage to locate a cast member who could sign Peter Pan's signature. After a lengthy search, the student obtained Peter Pan's autograph and gave it to the young boy. The student explained to the boy that Peter Pan wouldn't start the parade until he received his autograph. To add to the magic of the situation, the student's shift had concluded and he was about to be off the clock for the day, but he took the moment to create a magical moment for the young boy.

As the Magic Kingdom's day concluded one fall evening, a five year old girl ran up to a student and hugged his leg. The student knelt down, and the young guest thanked him for her magical day. The student was wearing a pair of "Mickey Hands" and gave them to her to wear. For thirty minutes, the young girl helped the student wave good night to guests exiting the park.

As one student swept the walkways in Fantasyland, he noticed a young boy crying because he just spilled a large bucket of popcorn onto the ground. Without hesitation, the student stopped sweeping and went to the nearest vendor to get a new bucket filled with popcorn. The student handed the new bucket to the young boy, and the excited boy dropped the bucket again so he could hug the student's leg.

A Fall, 2003 alumna states: "If you work in Operations you have the opportunity to work Parade Audience Control. I worked Magic Kingdom's Spectromagic a lot of nights and would bring kids out into the street before the lights went out. I'd choreograph it to the lights and music to where it seemed as if the kids turned the lights out, which signaled the start of the parade."

A Spring, 2004 alumnus remembers: "A family was unable to get tickets to the sold-out Magic Kingdom Christmas party, and it was their last night at the resort. They also had not visited the Magic Kingdom and still had one day left on their passes. I let the family into the park and told them to have a good time. Later in the evening, they requested to speak with me. They thanked me and gave me a large box of chocolates."

A Fall, 2004 alumna recalls: "A young girl and her family were leaving the Magic Kingdom but she had yet to meet Mickey Mouse. I knew Mickey Mouse was about to go onstage to wave good night to park guests, so I pulled him aside to a corner and called over the young girl. The girl and her family got to spend a few private moments with Mickey Mouse and they left the park with large smiles."

~

Guest and College Program student interactions make for other memorable moments at the Walt Disney World Resort. Tired and angry guests are known to ask some very unusual questions. Students try their best to respond with polite and appropriate answers. However, some high-maintenance guests deserve high-maintenance answers.

During one spring afternoon, a guest walking down Main Street U.S.A., looking straight at the park's only castle, asked where the castle was located. The perplexed student pointed toward the castle and the guest remarked, "No, the bigger castle in the park."

Another student was helping a guest exit the Haunted Mansion when a different guest asked if Disney knew the house was haunted. The student responded, "Of course Disney knows it's haunted; that's why we call it the Haunted Mansion."

One afternoon, a student stood at the entrance to Pirates of the Caribbean dressed in his full costume as a pirate when a guest asked if he worked there. The student replied, "No, I dress like a pirate for the hell of it!"

During a thunderstorm, one curious family asked how long the rain would be coming down. The student smiled and said, "Five minutes to five days. You better hurry up and take cover before it gets worse!" The family panicked and rushed out of the Magic Kingdom. The sun came out five minutes later.

Another intelligent guest asked how long foot-long hot dogs were. The student replied, "Twelve inches."

A rather bright guest asked a student working Parade Audience Control where a certain attraction was located.

"Excuse me, I can't seem to find a ride I've been looking for all day," said the guest.

The student replied, "Sure, I'll be glad to help."

"I've looked all over Fantasyland, and I can't find the Matterhorn."

"Um, I'm sorry, but you're mistaken; the Matterhorn is in Disneyland."

Showing the student his park map, "See, the Matterhorn is right there on the map!"

"This map is from Disneyland."

"But we rode it earlier this year. Did you guys move it to Disneyland?"

"No. We've never had the Matterhorn here at Walt Disney World."

"Well, I think you're lying!"

"I'm sorry sir but I'm not lying."

"Shit...let's go!"

A student working at the Magic Kingdom was asked where the fireworks would be displayed.

"In the sky," responded the student.

"But where?" asked the guest.

"Above the castle."

"Huh?"

"The fireworks will take place at the Orlando International Airport. Guest Relations will give you directions."

"Oh, ok. Thank you."

A group of guests asked what time the fireworks would begin. Incidentally, the fireworks were already five minutes into the show and still going off.

The student said, "Do you see those lights up in the sky? That would be them."

The guests looked surprised and ran as fast as they could to catch them.

During one summer afternoon, guests were lined up on the side of the street for the Magic Kingdom parade. A guest approached a student working Parade Audience Control.

The guest asked, "Is there a parade?"

"Nope, we just like to see how many people we can get to stand on the side of the street from time-to-time," responded the student.

Due to a severe lightning and thunderstorm, the outdoor attraction Test Track had to be shut down one spring afternoon.

A student made the announcement. "Due to the weather we are closing down this attraction, and it will reopen when the weather has improved."

"But why are you closing it?" asked a guest.

"There is lightning and thunder, and for safety reasons we are evacuating the attraction."

"But why can't I ride?"

"Because you'll get struck by lightning!"

"But why can't I ride?"

"How about this. I've always wondered what a person looks like when they get struck by lightning, so if you really want to ride, be my guest."

During a thunderstorm one fall afternoon, a student working in Fantasyland was asked if it was raining in Frontierland.

The student said, "It only rains here one land at a time."

"At what time will it stop raining in Fantasyland?" asked the guest.

"After we shut the rain off. About ten minutes from now."

"Great! Thank you!"

As a thunderstorm hit the Magic Kingdom during one fall afternoon, a guest approached a student.

"How dare you people. I'm on vacation!" yelled the guest.

"I'm not God," replied the student.

The guest was taken aback for a moment. "You can go to hell!"

The student smiled. "At least it won't be raining there."

In 2006, Pirates of the Caribbean was refurbished to include the addition of the film's Jack Sparrow character, played by Johnny Depp. The Johnny Depp addition to the attraction was so life-like that it left some guests confused after exiting the attraction.

"Excuse me, how do we get Johnny Depp's autograph?" asked a guest.

"Pardon me?" replied the student.

"Johnny Depp's autograph. We saw him in the ride and we want his autograph."

"I'm sorry, but those characters aren't real."

"Bullshit! It looked just like Johnny Depp!"

"That's the point."

"Well, I think you just want him all to yourself. I'm reporting you!"

The angry guest walked away as the student shook her head in disbelief.

A student working at the entrance to the Country Bear Jamboree had to give a guest a quick lesson on the differences between an attraction and a show.

"What kind of ride is this?" asked the guest.

"It's not a ride, it's a show," explained the student.

"Are there a lot of drops?"

"No, it's a show."

"So, is there any spinning?"

"No, again, this is a show; there is no movement!"

"This isn't where the kid died is it?"

"No, that was Mission: SPACE, and the child didn't die on the ride."

"So, this is a ride?"

"Yes, this is a ride and you may die on it!"

Some guests are clueless as to what they've just experienced. A guest walking out of the exit of Mission: SPACE approached a student.

"Excuse me, sir. Where's Mission: SPACE?" asked the guest.

"Um, sir, you just got off it," explained the student.

"Oh, thank you."

Other guests are so lost that they don't even remember where they were prior to boarding a ride. A guest getting off Mission: SPACE asked how he was to return to the theme park.

"Do we board another flight?" asked the guest.

"You didn't go anywhere," responded the student.

"We're on Mars right now, and I need to get back to earth. Do you speak Martian?"

"Sir, you're on Earth."

"But we landed on Mars."

"Fine...you have to get in that two-hour line again to return home."

"That's all I was asking! Sheesh!"

At Mission: SPACE, right before a family of six began boarding the attraction and after a ninety minute wait, the father stopped, and asked a rather odd question.

"Will this make me sick?" asked the guest.

"Well, are you prone to motion sickness?" asked the student.

"A little."

"Then it's a possibility."

"If I throw up, do I have to clean it up?"

"It's policy on Mars that you clean up your own mess."

"Wait...what ride is this?"

"Mission: SPACE."

"Shit, I thought this was Space Mountain! Why don't you people post signs in the front?"

The guest walked away with his family after they waited in a ninety minute line and without even riding the attraction.

One student was greeting guests at Epcot's Soarin' when a young lady requested directions.

"Where's the Tower of Terror?" asked the guest.

"Disney-MGM Studios," replied the student.

"No, the big scary ride that's supposed to drop you."

"Disney-MGM Studios."

"Thanks for the help. You're really creating the magic for me and my family!"

During one busy holiday season, the lines became pretty lengthy at Epcot's Soarin'.

"Why is the wait ninety minutes?" asked a guest.

The student calmly replied, "Because it's a busy day here at Epcot."

"Why's it busy?"

"Because it's Thanksgiving week."

"Is it really ninety minutes?"

"Nope, we're instructed to lie to you!"

"Why's there a lot of people in line?"

Irritated with the questions the student said, "We're busy today, so please leave me alone!"

After park hours concluded at Epcot, a student was covering the turnstiles with tarps at Test Track when a guest walked up and tried getting in line for the attraction.

"I'm sorry sir, we're closed for the night," said the student.

"Really, what time did you close tonight?" asked the guest.

"Nine o'clock."

"My watch says eight; I think you have the wrong time."

"Sir, I know its past nine because Illuminations is going off."

"Are you sure they aren't at eight?"

"Positive."

"But my watch says eight."

"Sir, you do know that Florida is in a different time zone?"

"Huh?"

After riding Test Track, a guest wanted a little more information about the ride and made an unusual request.

"Excuse me, were we supposed to be the crash test dummies?" asked the guest.

"Well, that's kind of the storyline," replied the student.

"So, are you calling us dummies?"

"No, not at all."

"Oh. Could I drive my car on the Test Track?"

"Um, this is a ride."

"Why can't I test my car on the Test Track?"

"Sir, it's against policy."

"Listen, I'm no dummy. It's called Test Track, so I should be able to test my car on the track!"

"Okay, sir. Go right ahead."

"Well, my car is in California, so how am I supposed to test it?"

Wanting to bang his head on a wall, the patient student smiled. "You could always rent a car."

"Well, there's no point then. It would have to be my own car to test," replied the guest.

The student smiled again and walked away in disbelief.

EARNING

A student working at Disney's Animal Kingdom's Dinosaur had to deal with a very bright and intellectual group of teenagers during one hot summer afternoon.

"Excuse me, where's the Jurassic Park ride?" asked the group.

"That's at Universal Studios. We have the Dinosaur ride. Just head to your right and you'll get there," explained the student.

"But we wanna go on the Jurassic Park ride."

"We don't have that ride in Walt Disney World. We only have the Dinosaur ride."

"Will they have it at the Magic Kingdom?"

"No. Walt Disney World doesn't have a Jurassic Park ride, only Dinosaur. You need to go to Universal Studios, which is not a Disney Park, and is about twenty minutes away if you exit Walt Disney World and head East on I-4."

"Oh, so where's that ride again?"

Working at Pleasure Island can provide some very entertaining guests who have consumed large amounts of alcohol. As one student discovered, some guests don't need alcohol to display acts of pure stupidity.

"Is this City Walk?" asked a guest.

"No, this is Pleasure Island...nightclubs and a street party atmosphere, where it's New Year's Eve every night," explained the student.

"Oh, well, where's City Walk?"

"That's Universal Studios."

"Oh, do the Disney buses take me there?"

"No, the Disney buses only take you around Disney property."

"Then why don't they take me to Universal Studios?"

"Because they're Universal, they aren't part of Disney."

"Oh, so how will I get to City Walk?"

"Take I-4 toward Orlando and follow the signs."

"Where do the buses pick me up at?"

"The buses to the Disney Resorts and theme parks?"

"No, to City Walk."

"We don't have buses that go to City Walk!"

"How much is this Pleasure Island thing? I'll take two tickets."

In a separate incident, a guest approached a student working at the Pleasure Island ticket window and asked a common question.

"I'll take two tickets to Disney Island," requested the guest.

"Sir, this is Pleasure Island," explained the student.

"Oh, where's Disney Island?"

"We don't have a Disney Island."

"Why would you have an island of sex at Walt Disney World?"

"Sex?"

"Well, you said this was Pleasure Island."

"Sir, this is an island of nightclubs, restaurants and shops."

"So, it's Disney Island?"

"Yes, it's Disney Island."

While working in the Main Street U.S.A. Emporium, a student was approached by a guest asking for medication.

"Do you carry Children's Advil?" asked the guest.

"No, we only carry Children's Tylenol," replied the student.

"Well, I'm a Pediatrician and I know that Children's Advil is better than Tylenol. Why don't you carry it? That's unacceptable!"

"Well, if you're a doctor, and you know Children's Advil is better, why didn't you bring some with you?"

While working at an Outdoor Vending Cart, a student was asked about Walt Disney World's policy on robbery.

"Have you ever been robbed before?" asked the guest.

"I personally haven't but I know it has happened," answered the student.

"What happens when a robbery does occur?"

"We normally have a sniper on the roof, usually Donald Duck, and he takes out the thief at the first opportunity."

"Yeah, I heard about that on the news."

"Oh really? That's not good." The student got on his two-way radio. "Donald, we have a target. I repeat…we have a target."

The guest ran away from the cart.

During one hot summer afternoon at Epcot, a guest couldn't comprehend a certain level of information due to the heat.

"Excuse me, I'm looking for a ride," said the guest.

"Which ride are you looking for?" asked the student.

"I'm looking for Lord of the Dance."

"Oh, that's a show, not a ride."

"That's what I said, I said a show…Yes, a show."

"Well, that show is playing over at the American Pavilion."

"What show?"

"Lord of the Dance."

"What's Lord of the Dance?"

"The show you requested."

"Huh?"

The student couldn't continue with the conversation because he was unaware of how to respond. "I don't think I can help you."

"All I asked was where Lord of the Dance was located."

"American Pavilion."

"Why didn't you say that in the first place? Shit…you Disney people!"

A lost and confused guest asked where a particular attraction was located and how to get to the attraction.

"Where's Expedition Matterhorn?" asked the guest.

"Do you mean Expedition Everest?" questioned the student.

"No, Expedition Matterhorn."

"We have Expedition Everest, which is here at Disney's Animal Kingdom."

"Oh, can I board a helicopter to get there?"

"Um, no. You'd have to walk."

"Excuse me? I'm not walking to Asia."

"Sir, it's right around the corner."

"Listen, I wasn't born yesterday. I know Mt. Everest is in Asia and Asia is in London, which is a half-day trip from here."

"Okay sir, I apologize. I'll inform Mickey Mouse to prepare the resort helicopter."

While working as a Custodial Host in the Magic Kingdom, a guest made an unusual complaint.

"Do you work here?" asked the guest.

"Yes I do," replied the student as he looked at his white costume.

"My ice cream just melted."

"It's ninety degrees out here. It'll do that."

"I want a new one."

"Sure. Let me help you with that. Be right back."

"I want four extra cones for my family, too."

"I can only replace the one."

"Bullshit! If you can do one, you can get me four extra ones!"

"I'm sorry, I can't do that."

"Forget it! I'll be reporting you to customer relations."

The award for the best student and guest interaction occurred in Spring, 2003 at the World of Disney store in Downtown Disney. The student's work location was Space Mountain in the Magic Kingdom.

"Do you work here?" asked the guest.

"No," replied the student.

"Do you carry DVD's?"

"I don't know. I don't work here!"

"What about CD's?"

"I still have no idea. I don't work here! I'm shopping! Ask someone who works here!"

"Well, why'd you tell me you worked here?"

"I didn't! If you would have turned your mouth off and turned your ears on, you would have heard me two minutes ago!"

"How rude!"

The student's roommate approached and asked, "Hey, where's the sweatshirts?"

"Around the corner," answered the student.

Overhearing the conversation, the upset guest said, "I'm reporting you to your manager! You said you didn't work here! What's your name, and what's your manager's name?"

The student calmly answered, "My name is Anthony, and my manager doesn't work here. He works at my job, where I work, which isn't here! I don't work here!"

"Well, you won't work here when I'm done talking to your manager!"

"Hey lady, go scare someone who cares!"

~

The Walt Disney World Resort consists of theme parks, attractions, hotels, live entertainment, restaurant experiences and more, but it is the College Program students and cast members who make it all possible for guests to experience. Without their smiling faces, hard work, and dedication, the Walt Disney World Resort wouldn't exist. After long days working in a role, which pays very little, and maintaining the Disney mindset, students are capable of surviving while they work for the Mouse.

Chapter Five

Living

Childishness? I think it's the equivalent of never losing your sense of humor. I mean, there's a certain something that you retain. It's the equivalent of not getting so stuffy that you can't laugh at others.
—Walt Disney

A typical day in the life of a College Program student consists of waking up at noon, sitting by the pool, going to work late in the afternoon, getting off work around midnight, partying until the early morning hours, and then trying to get at least four hours of sleep before it's repeated all over again. Living while in the program is probably one of the greatest social experiences one can have. Learning to live with others and socializing with people from all backgrounds is the most beneficial component of the entire program. The *Living* experience can be adventurous and definitely challenging for every student.

Students take up residence at Vista Way, Chatham Square, The Commons, or Patterson Court apartment complexes. Rent is taken directly out of students' paychecks each week. All utilities, including electricity, are included. Not having to pay an electrical bill is a benefit due to the central air-conditioning constantly being operated in the warm climate. Students' rights are strictly limited, and they can be forced to leave due to any infraction with only a twenty-four hour notice.

The Vista Way apartment complex opened in 1988 and is the main complex where students are housed. The Commons complex opened in 1998, the Chatham Square complex opened in 2000, and Patterson Court opened its gates in 2008. The Commons, Chatham Square, and Patterson Court are all located in the same area (about one mile from Vista Way). Most students request to live in the newer and more moderate Chatham Square, The Commons, or Patterson Court complexes in lieu of the older Vista Way. Vista Way generally runs near full occupancy as management tends to fill this complex before the other two locations. Historically, students living at Vista Way are provided with the most memorable social experiences while in the program. With that being said, the following discussions will be focused on Vista Way, or as some call it, *Vista Lay*.

~

Two to three bedroom fully furnished apartments are provided and each is based on dual occupancy. The bedrooms include beds, dressers and mirrors. The living room includes a couch, easy chair, coffee table, and two end tables. The kitchen includes sets of plates, cups, mugs, utensils, and appliances. High speed Internet is provided in each apartment as well. Students have access to laundry facilities, cable television, weight rooms, tennis and basketball courts, and computer labs.

LIVING

Some students furnish the apartment with their own items, or at least attempt to. Two students purchased a thirty inch wide-screen television and carried it up to their third floor apartment. They opened the box and discovered the television's side had been cracked. They carried the television back down the stairs and returned it to the store. After getting a second television, they carried it back up the stairs and into their apartment. After opening the box, they discovered the television's screen had a scratch across the front. The two students yet again had to carry the heavy television back down the stairs so they could make the return. After getting a third television and having learned their lesson, they opened the box while inside the store. The television was free from damages. The two students returned to the complex and carried the television back up the stairs. When they reached the third floor, they lost their grip and dropped the television over the balcony. They finally gave up and had the store make the fourth delivery to their apartment.

Learning how to properly operate kitchen appliances can be challenging for students who normally rely on their parents. Looking confused in the kitchen, one student asked his roommate, "Which one's the stove?"

Another student asked his roommate how to "cook ice." The roommate asked if he meant, "Make ice," but he really wanted to know how ice was cooked. The confused roommate suggested the stove, but the inquiring student said, "It will melt on the stove."

During one fall evening, a student was almost certain aluminum could be used in the microwave. Within seconds, he quickly learned going out to eat would be safer. There were only minor damages to the kitchen area, and the students weren't injured.

Thinking liquid Dawn dish soap would work in a dishwasher, four students learned quite the opposite. After returning home from dinner, the students were welcomed to a kitchen and living room full of soapsuds. Not quite sure if they ever used the dishwasher again.

A Spring, 2000 alumna recalls: "Nobody would take the trash out and it just piled up all over the place. The trash piled up to almost the kitchen ceiling and wasn't taken out until management inspected our apartment."

A Fall, 2002 alumnus remembers: "One night we took all of our furniture and tried stacking it to the ceiling. About half way, the tall stack of furniture fell and almost wiped out one of our roommates."

A Spring, 2005 alumnus recalls: "My roommates and I were so poor that we had to steal rolls of toilet paper from the bathrooms at work."

~

Vista Way management operates out of the clubhouse, a main building on property. Here, students can file complaints, make work-order requests, mail large packages, pick up packages, and borrow cleaning supplies such as vacuums, brooms, and mops.

Filing complaints are common among students, but every now and then there are complaints that are far from common. One student filed a complaint stating that he woke up in the middle of the night and discovered that his roommate was standing at the side of his bed staring at him. The strange roommate was relocated to another apartment.

Another student filed a complaint because his roommate asked him if he wanted to lick the chicken grease off his fingers.

Needless to say, the student didn't lick the chicken grease and was relocated to another apartment.

In yet another odd complaint, a student complained that his two homosexual roommates were having sex every night in the kitchen. The student was relocated, but ironically, three weeks later his new roommate caught him having sex in the kitchen. The ironic incident grew larger as he was having sex with his new roommate's girlfriend. The two students engaged in a physical altercation and both were terminated from the program.

Work-orders are submitted daily and some requests require extensive attention, while other requests only require the use of one's brain. A confused student filed a work-order which indicated the shower had no hot water. Maintenance visited the apartment for an inspection and found nothing wrong with the plumbing. Maintenance suggested that the shower fixture be turned to hot for hot water.

Another student submitted a work-order stating the refrigerator in his apartment wasn't working. Maintenance inspected the refrigerator and discovered there was no electricity being supplied to the unit. The student inquired as to what the problem was and maintenance explained that the refrigerator needed to be plugged in and remained plugged in for it to work.

A Fall, 1997 alumna recalls: "My roommate snored really loud, and I asked to be relocated to a new apartment. Management informed me I couldn't relocate to a new location. I was so upset that I decided to fill out a work-order, which asked for maintenance to come and fix my roommate's snoring. Two days later, management relocated my roommate instead of me."

MOUSECATRAZ

A Spring, 1998 alumna remembers: "Our air-conditioner wouldn't work. We'd turn it to cool, but an hour later the apartment would be hot. After talking with maintenance we learned there was nothing broken. We learned that one of our roommates would turn the heat on after she came home because it was too cold for her. It was ninety degrees outside and she was cold. She finally moved out and we froze our apartment in celebration to the point where ice could have formed."

A Fall, 2000 alumnus recalls: "I borrowed a vacuum and took it to my apartment. My roommate knew how to operate a vacuum but not on a carpet. He vacuumed the kitchen floor. I had to explain that the broom and mop were for the kitchen floor and the vacuum was for the carpet."

~

Visitors are allowed on property with strict guidelines enforced. Students must sign-in their visitors at the security entrance. Visitors are prohibited from the complex after 1:00 A.M., which means overnight visitors aren't allowed. Students violating the visitor policy are terminated from the program. Around-the-clock security is provided to maintain a safe environment. Whether driving an automobile or walking by foot, students are required to display their housing identification card upon entering the tightly secured complex.

Random automobile searches are conducted, and some searches result in unique findings. During one vehicle search, security discovered twelve cases of beer in an under-aged student's vehicle. The student was terminated from the program.

In a separate incident, a student drove up to the complex's entrance and was asked by security to open his trunk. The trunk was popped open, and two female students from the Chatham Square complex jumped out and ran away as fast as they could.

The student tried his best to sneak his female friends into the complex after curfew. The students weren't terminated from the program.

Another student's vehicle was searched, and three marijuana plants were found in the back seat. Not stopping there, a small bag of cocaine was located above the passenger side visor. The student was turned over to the local police authorities, and the student never returned to the program.

A Spring, 1999 alumnus remembers: "A security guard observed me pouring a substance from a red gasoline can onto the bushes around my apartment building. It appeared that I was trying to set the building on fire, but I informed the security guard that it was only water."

A Fall, 2000 alumnus recalls: "Security personnel informed me that I was terminated from the program. I had no idea what I had done, but just knew I had to turn in my key and ID by noon on the following day. After turning in my key and ID, I learned it was because my under-aged roommate had alcohol in our wellness apartment and we were all held accountable."

A Spring, 2001 alumna remembers: "My friend and I walked past a security guard and I said 'shit' to my friend. The security guard stopped us and lectured us about using profanity. We pretty much told him to 'screw off.'"

A Fall, 2003 alumna recalls: "There was a thunderstorm and a security guard walked me from the buses to my apartment. On our way, lightning struck a light pole about ten-feet from us. We jumped, ran another way and lightning struck yet another light pole about ten-feet away from us. We were dodging attacks and I believe that was the last time we were outside during a thunderstorm."

~

Transportation is provided for students through a private company. Shuttle buses offer hourly trips to the Walt Disney World Resort work locations and a few selected shopping centers. The central hub for the buses is located at the front of Vista Way property. Students not having an automobile while in the program try their best to avoid riding the old shuttle buses by carpooling with friends and co-workers. A ride on a Vista Way shuttle bus can make for an entertaining, but also social, experience for most students. For several years, Dynamic provided the bus services. The Dynamic buses were well known for breaking down and falling apart. With that said, the following discussions will focus on students' experiences with the Dynamic buses.

The Dynamic bus transporting students to and from Pleasure Island generally fills up to standing room only. During one late night bus ride home from Pleasure Island, a student couldn't control his vomiting. Before the bus could return to the apartment complex, the seats, floor, windows, and several other students were drenched in a hefty amount of protein spill.

After returning from Pleasure Island late one night, a brave student decided to get back on the bus and into the driver's seat. As the intoxicated student drove away, security personnel flagged down the bus and stopped the student before he could drive any further. The student was immediately terminated from the program. The student worked in Transportation while in the program, but he apparently couldn't get enough of his work.

The Dynamic bus drivers were notorious for getting lost and ending up in unusual locations. After picking up a small group of students from Disney's Animal Kingdom, the bus driver decided to make a quick stop at the nearby Post Office and Kinko's. The driver needed to complete a few errands before he dropped the students off at Vista Way.

During one journey to the Magic Kingdom, the driver got lost somewhere on the roads near Disney's Fort Wilderness Lodge. After driving around in circles for about thirty minutes, the bus finally gave up and broke down. Students were stranded for another thirty minutes until another bus could pick them up.

Another adventurous bus was on its way back from the Magic Kingdom, taking students home to Vista Way. To the students' surprise, they ended up at Sea World by mistake.

A Spring, 2001 alumna remembers: "It was common for the Dynamic buses to break down. We were on our way to the Magic Kingdom when our bus broke down. After being stranded for about twenty minutes, we started walking the long route. Most of us survived the three mile walk, but were about one hour late for our shifts."

Another Spring, 2001 alumna recalls: "The Dynamic buses were death traps and a tragedy waiting to happen. We never knew where we'd end up. One day, we were supposed to arrive at Epcot, but were taken to Downtown Disney instead. The driver couldn't understand English, so we were all pretty much stranded for a while."

A Spring, 2003 alumna remembers: "I was talking with my friend on the bus and a cockroach fell into her hair. I screamed, she screamed and the bus pulled over to the side of the road. After the driver learned what we were screaming about, he tried accelerating the bus and couldn't because the bus broke down. He should have never stopped the bus."

A Spring, 2003 alumnus recalls: "Managers knew our buses broke down often, so if we were ever late for a shift, most students just blamed it on the buses."

A Fall, 2003 alumnus remembers: "None of the bus drivers could speak English. We'd ask them a question and hearing their response would be like hearing marbles move around in their mouths."

A Fall, 2004 alumnus states: "I think everyone has been almost hit by a Dynamic or Vista Way bus at least one time. The drivers are crazy. To this date, I still can't figure out what language the drivers spoke."

A Spring, 2005 alumnus recalls: "We were on our way to work when we passed another Dynamic bus sitting on the side of the road. Several students were standing around and as we passed the front of the bus, I saw a body covered by a blanket. The bus actually hit and killed something or someone. It wasn't the Dynamic bus' fault, but it just reiterated how the buses were like death on wheels."

A Spring, 2005 alumna remembers: "One of the Dynamic buses blew up. I was over at the Chatham complex and heard a large explosion. I saw the bus and all of the windows were covered in black from the smoke. Most of the bus was in pieces but nobody was hurt."

Another Spring, 2005 alumna recalls: "I think I needed counseling after riding the Dynamic buses for a year. How we survived those bus rides remains a mystery."

~

Learning to accommodate roommates can be the most challenging component of the *Living* experience for students. Bothersome quirks, annoying routines, laziness, personal hygiene, and tolerance are all obstacles to overcome while living with fellow roommates. Simple chores such as taking the garbage out, cleaning up after a mess is made, or making a bed can all be difficult for some to accomplish.

Getting along with each other and socializing like a family makes the *Living* experience much more enriching. During one spring evening, a water balloon fight between two apartment buildings was in full force until a security guard got pegged in the face. To the students' surprise, the security guard grabbed a filled water balloon from the ground and launched it at a student standing on the third floor, smacking him in the face.

During a separate water balloon battle, students on the third floor would launch water balloons onto passing students down below. Aware of what was occurring, another student walked past the targeted area but quickly released a water balloon of his own onto the third floor.

Not having much to do during one fall evening, two roommates decided to use a plate as a frisbee. After several tosses, one missed its target and smacked another roommate in the side of his face, knocking out two of his teeth. The student was rushed to urgent care by his roommate.

During a rather slow evening at home, four male roommates decided to display their bare butts up against their third floor window. Passing students looking up at the window would see nothing but a line of full moons.

One evening, a group of female students stood out in front of their apartment building and flashed their breasts at passing drivers. One male student was so distracted that he crashed his car into a light pole. The flashers immediately vacated the area, and the unlucky driver was stuck with damages to his brand new Lexus.

One late night, four female roommates tried their skills at building a fort. Using mattresses, furniture, blankets, and everything else possible, they created a fort that covered the entire apartment. The fort was so large and complex that one of the students got lost while inside the fort and screamed for one of her roommates to come and rescue her.

While playing videogames during one afternoon, two students decided to try something a little different. They grabbed their lawn chairs, faced the television toward the window, and sat outside in the warm sun while they played.

One night, several students attempted to see how many bodies they could fit into a single bathroom. After squeezing twenty people into the bathroom, an unknown culprit let off a stink bomb and turned the event into a mad scramble to break out of the cramped space. Nobody was hurt during the mad scramble.

A Spring, 1998 alumna remembers: "We loved pillow fights and one night I smacked my roommate in the face with a pillow and it sent feathers everywhere."

A Fall, 2000 alumnus recalls: "We'd pull our mattresses off of the beds and have mattress rides down the stairs. We'd set the mattress on the steps, get a running start, and leap onto the mattress. The furthest one down from their jump would win."

~

Pranks among students are popular and effective strategies in building relationships with fellow roommates. Pranks create such a strong rapport among students that when they do occur, most students welcome the spirited nature. One student duct taped his bedroom doorway while his roommate was sound asleep. The sleeping roommate woke up, opened the door, and walked into the sticky trap. The tangled roommate fell to the ground and struggled to break free as his three roommates laughed at his expense.

While using the bathroom in the middle of the night, a female student learned that saran wrap becomes unnoticeable when wrapped around the toilet bowl. The shocked student made quite a mess to say the least.

In one prank, two students filled their roommate's pillowcase with popcorn. As their intoxicated roommate stumbled in late that night, he laid his head on the pillow, only to get a startling and crunchy surprise.

Late one night a female student pulled back her bed sheets and discovered what appeared to be three used condoms. After her disgruntled reaction and hearing her roommates laughing in the other room, she learned that the condoms were filled with shampoo.

During one clever prank, a female student approached the entrance to her apartment and discovered the entrance had been roped off with yellow caution tape and a chalk outline of a body was drawn on the concrete. The terrified student ran away from the apartment as her laughing roommates stepped out of the apartment from across the hall. After the prank the students wrote "CP" inside the chalk outline, giving the impression that a College Program student had been murdered.

A Fall, 1998 alumnus recalls: "We hid all of the toilet paper we had in the apartment and when it came time for our roommate needing some, we heard a loud 'help!' "

A Spring, 2001 alumnus remembers: "I placed jelly in my roommate's bed. He came home late and jumped into bed.

Completely exhausted, he didn't even realize he was sleeping with strawberry jelly. I woke up the next morning and he had already left. After showering, I went to put my socks on and they were jammed with strawberry jelly. He also put jelly in my shoes and hat. He got the last laugh."

~

Every building at Vista Way has laundry facilities for students to use. The card-operated machines are located on the ground floor and students quickly learn that laundry isn't done through magic. Once students realize that their mothers aren't there to wash their clothes, they have to learn the fundamentals of a washer and dryer. In lieu of laundry detergent, one student used dish soap to wash his clothing. The unpleasant soap worked but resulted in an allergic reaction and several days of constant scratching.

Another student learned what happens when excessive laundry detergent is used as he used an entire three-quart bottle of detergent for one load of laundry. The laundry room for his building overflowed with soapsuds.

After not being able to start the washing machine, one impatient student decided that kicking the machine would be more effective. After a few kicks and punches, a security guard caught the student and inquired about the assault on the machine. After hearing the explanation of the machine not working, the security guard suggested pushing the start button. The student said, "Oh, I forgot to do that."

A Fall, 2001 alumnus recalls: "I never did my laundry before I was in the program. The first time I did my laundry I washed my reds with my whites and ended up with bright pink shirts."

LIVING

A Spring, 2004 alumnus remembers: "All the washing machines were occupied one day and I didn't have any clean clothes to wear. I took someone else's clothes out of a washing machine, piled them in the corner and started washing my clothes. When I went back down to put my wet clothes in the dryer, I discovered they had been scattered all over the grass."

~

The swimming pool and hot tub are popular hangouts at Vista Way. Students gather to enjoy the warm sun and socialize with fellow students. Beautiful women in two-piece bathing suits cool off in the refreshing blue water as their male counterparts try their best to catch a glimpse. During one evening of admiring a group of female students wearing their two-piece bikinis, the student wasn't paying attention to where he was walking and walked straight into the pool.

After rubbing sunscreen on the backs of five beautiful female students, a lucky student got up and turned around to discover that his girlfriend had witnessed his friendly gestures. His girlfriend gave him a black eye and shoved him into the pool. It must not have been that big of a deal because they remained together for the duration of the program.

During a thunderstorm, one student believed it was safe for him to go swimming. Not thinking twice about why no one else was in the pool or why the gates were closed, he swam all alone until security escorted him out of the pool for safety precautions.

During one late summer night, fifteen students decided to swim in the nude. After thirty minutes of skinny-dipping, the party was interrupted when two spying students arrived at the pool and began taking several pictures of the skinny-dippers. After a few moments of chaos, the photographers fled the scene and the photographs were never recovered.

MOUSECATRAZ

A Spring, 2005 alumna recalls: "It was 3:00 A.M. when my friends and I decided it would be funny to sneak into the pool. After climbing over the fence and dropping cameras, hairpieces and money during the process, we stripped off our clothes and jumped in. Four security guards arrived, shined their flashlights on us and said 'Get out of the pool.' As my friends were getting out of the pool, I was running around the pool waving the bras and thongs in the air. The security guards snapped the lock off the gate with pliers and purposely blamed that on us as well. Security interrogated us for over two hours."

~

A variety of athletic opportunities at the complex such as tennis, racquetball, basketball, and volleyball are available. Students participate in basketball tournaments, grueling tennis matches and barbecue outings with a friendly game of volleyball on the sandy court. After losing a grueling tennis match, a student tossed his racquet out of frustration and the flying racquet landed in a nearby car windshield. The student quickly retrieved his racquet and pretended nothing ever happened. Later that night, the student's roommate came home and was clearly angry. The student learned that the car windshield he'd broken belonged to his roommate. Having an honest conscience, the student explained to his roommate what had happened and gave him the money for the necessary repairs.

During a highly competitive, old-fashioned street basketball game, one student broke his leg. Surprisingly, the student continued playing until the alpha-unit arrived ten minutes later to take him away.

During one spring evening, a group of students decided to barbecue hamburgers and hot dogs for their friendly game of volleyball. As the food cooked on the grill, they played their game. Suddenly, a small fire broke out on the ground around the barbecue. Unaware of how such a blaze could have started, the students quickly discovered that a bird had attempted to steal their food but caught fire instead. The bird survived, and the students ate grilled burgers instead of grilled bird.

A Fall, 2000 alumnus remembers: "After a highly competitive volleyball game one evening, a brawl broke out among all of the players. After it was all over I learned that the brawl had nothing to do with the game but with one of the guys who had played. Apparently, he had slept with four of the opposing players' girlfriends during the previous week."

A Spring, 2003 alumnus recalls: "A group of us would run our own basketball tournament. There was a group of girls who'd hang out at all of the games and act as cheerleaders. During one of the games, a girl came out onto the court and showed a bunch of the guys up. She was tougher than most of them and from then on, she was on my team."

~

Kegs of beer, party balls, destructive or disruptive behavior, and drinking games all symbolize the alcoholic adventures of students in the program. One energetic student decided to swim across a pond on Vista Way property at 3:00 A.M. According to his friends, he had a little too much to drink during the evening and was attempting to impress a group of female students. Unfortunately for the swimmer, one of the female students needed to rescue him from drowning.

In a separate incident, an intoxicated student swam across a Vista Way pond. As a joke, a spectator yelled alligator, and the student started swimming even faster to the nearby land.

Late one night, two intoxicated students decided to spray shaving cream on parked cars. They continued spraying until they came across a vehicle where two students were making-out in the back seat. The students continued spraying the lovers' entire automobile with shaving cream without being caught.

At the start of six roommates' program, they purchased seventy-five cases of Budweiser and stored the cases in their closet. They maintained the supply throughout their program and would never let it go below fifty cases. The cases didn't go to waste because on their last night the students finished off over fifty cases of Budweiser during a party.

Students host themed parties including Graffiti, TOGA, Hawaiian, Playboy, Pajama, and Mardi Gras. Drinking games such as Beer Pong, Asshole, Power Hour, Body Shots, and Thumper are all classics among students. After attending a classic party the night before, one sick student couldn't miss any more days at work. The student went to work and after only ten minutes of working, he informed his manager he needed to go home. The student suddenly vomited all over his manager's white shirt. The manager needed no further explanation and sent the student home.

In a separate incident, one student knew there would be a massive party later in the evening and requested an Early Release from work. The manager asked for a reason and the student said, "So I can go home and get drunk!" He was Early Released.

A Fall, 1997 alumna recalls: "We'd do Body Shots in the middle of the walkways at Pleasure Island. We didn't need to be inside Vista Way to do some pretty wild stunts."

A Spring, 1999 alumnus remembers: "Late night parties and all-you-could-drink alcohol were the routine for most nights. One night, my roommates and I decided to play a game of monopoly, but after thirty minutes of playing, we turned the board game into a drinking game."

A Fall, 2002 alumnus recalls: "My roommate passed out on the couch during a party, so we picked him up and moved him to a friend's apartment over at The Commons complex. After waking up, he had no idea where he was and was clueless as to how he ended up a mile away."

A Spring, 2004 alumna remembers: "We were having a party and I went to use the bathroom but some guy had his head in the toilet bowl. After vomiting, he pulled his head up and to my surprise I learned that it was my manager from work."

A Fall, 2005 alumnus recalls: "We'd set up our beer bong on the third floor balcony and have it go all the way down to the first floor."

A Spring, 2006 alumna remembers: "Just to play it safe, we'd host the really wild parties at a local hotel and sometimes even a Disney-owned hotel. Partying, alcohol, sex, and hundreds of people made the events a crazy experience."

~

Girls running around in bikinis all day, good looking guys, hot and humid weather, and raging hormones are all key factors in turning Vista Way into *Vista Lay*. Sex occurs at Vista Way more often than probably any college campus or college town in the world. It's no secret that behind the walls of Vista Way, the sexual encounters, mishaps, and crazy experiences do exist.

Threesomes or more are common while in the program, and as one male student learned, dreams do come true. The student had a threesome with the students who played Alice, Snow

White, and Belle. The student who played Ariel found out what had occurred and was jealous, so the following night she had a one-on-one with the male student. Interestingly, the lucky male student was not a Character Performer nor a Lifeguard, but a simple and ordinary Custodial Host who worked at Downtown Disney.

During one late night, a male student was asleep when his roommate and his girlfriend came into the room. The two began having sex on the sleeping student's bed. After a few minutes, the sleeping student became involved in a threesome.

In a separate incident, one student couldn't get into his bedroom because the door was locked. After sleeping on the couch, morning had arrived and the door opened. Coming out of the room was one girl after another until finally, the tenth girl exited the room. Either his roommate was one lucky guy or someone who had just struck out ten times.

Relationships during a student's program rarely evolve into long-term commitments as the short program duration makes it difficult to achieve. Many students take full advantage of such a notion. As one male student slept in his bed, a female student crawled into his bed thinking he was her boyfriend. The two had sex and she turned the light on, only to realize she just had sex with her boyfriend's roommate by mistake. The female student got up and put her index finger to her lips and said, "Shhh! Don't tell John." The two never spoke of the incident ever again.

After having sex with a beautiful and busty female student, one male student asked if he'd be seeing her again. She informed him that he wouldn't be seeing her again because she had a boyfriend back home and that she just needed a quick fix.

Another student dated a girl for three weeks but never knew her name. The relationship ended after he used the wrong name while the two were having sex. As his upset ex-girlfriend walked out of the room, he asked her if she even knew his name. She couldn't answer and quickly left, resulting in two lovers who remained nameless to each other.

In the middle of having sex, a male student told his female partner that she was no good at having sex and requested to try her roommate. The male student left the room and went into the living room where the roommate was watching television. Five minutes later, the two had sex on the couch. A price was paid, however. The following morning, both his and the roommate's car tires were slashed.

One clever student dated four separate girls all named Lisa. He separated the four girls by naming them Lisa One, Lisa Two, Lisa Three, and Lisa Four. When asked one night who he was going out with for the evening he said, "L2 tonight and I'll see L4 tomorrow."

Some sexual interactions occur in full view of the public as some students just can't wait until the privacy of their own room. A group of students went to start up a volleyball game one evening and to their surprise, two students were having sex in the middle of the sandy court. The group began playing their game, and the two lovers scrambled out of the area.

One afternoon, a female student approached the laundry room and had the pleasure of witnessing two students having sex on a washing machine. After a closer look at who the female participant was, she discovered it was her younger sister who was visiting her while on vacation from New York. Adding to the awkward encounter, the male participant was none other than the student's boyfriend.

In a separate incident, one student had the pleasure of hearing his two male roommates having sex in the other room as they were quite loud. The following morning, the students in the apartment from below knocked on the door and asked if there was a cat stuck in the vent. Apparently, the entire apartment building heard what sounded like a wounded cat.

One unlucky student had to sleep on the couch because his bedroom door was locked. He assumed his roommate was having sex with his girlfriend. When morning arrived, he learned that his roommate was alone in the bedroom and had mistakenly locked the door.

During a bus ride home from the Magic Kingdom late one night, two students couldn't wait to express their physical attraction for each other. The two had sex in the back of the bus without anyone in the front ever knowing what was occurring. The two had just met ten minutes prior to having sex. According to the female student, it was the fact that her lover played Tigger and she just had a thing for Tigger.

A Fall, 1999 alumnus remembers: "My roommate was hard core religious, but after two weeks in the program he started sleeping with every girl he invited back to our apartment. I don't think I've ever seen anyone 'turn' so fast like he did."

A Spring, 2001 alumnus states: "I was very shy before I did the program. I couldn't even approach a girl just to say hello. After a week in the program, I opened up and began talking with every girl possible. After passing through the security entrance one evening, the girl with me couldn't wait any longer and hopped on my lap as I drove throughout the complex. I pulled into a parking space, we finished and said our good-byes. One hour later, I was in my room with a different girl."

A Spring, 2003 alumnus recalls: "I'd sleep with a different girl every week because I worked at Pleasure Island. I'd let all of the beautiful women in for free and they'd hang around me for the rest of the night."

A Fall, 2003 alumna remembers: "I went out to the pool one night and discovered a group orgy occurring in the hot tub. They didn't care who was watching or swimming in the pool."

A Spring, 2004 alumna recalls: "Everyone knew not to go in the hot tub because it was a prime location for couples to have sex in. I witnessed it at least three times. Some said it was a tub full of sexually transmitted diseases just waiting to find its next victim."

A Fall, 2004 alumna states: "There are a few women who have boyfriends back home, but some of them dump their boyfriends so they can enjoy as many men as possible while in the program."

A Spring, 2005 alumnus states: "If a girl gets pregnant at Vista Way, everyone calls it a 'Vista Way Baby.' No telling how many of those are roaming the earth."

A Spring, 2005 alumna states: "Vista Way = A lot of sex!"

A Fall, 2005 alumnus recalls: "I woke up in the middle of the night to get a glass of juice. I went out to the kitchen and my roommate and his girlfriend were having sex on the kitchen table. I got the glass of juice and returned to my room as they continued on. I think they knew I was passing through but didn't care."

A Spring, 2006 alumnus remembers: "I was laying in my bed one night when my roommate and his girlfriend came into the room. They assumed I was sleeping and began having sex. After twenty seconds, they were finished. I couldn't help it, so I began clapping. She was embarrassed and left the room. He tried telling me that he 'went longer' than twenty seconds but I knew otherwise."

A Spring, 2006 alumna states: "I think everyone in the program 'makes out' with at least one person. I made out with several guys, which half of them I hated beforehand."

~

Vista Way myths and legends do circulate among students each year. Some myths and legends are so mysterious that only a select few students are aware they exist. Whether or not the myths are true, each myth provides interesting conversations among past and present students.

After a late night party at a neighbor's apartment, a student returned to his apartment. The drunk and tired student stumbled into his bathroom, only to discover his roommate had hanged himself from the ceiling. The myth circulates among some students each year, but there is no record of a student hanging himself at a Vista Way apartment while in the program. Besides, it's very difficult to hang oneself from a bathroom ceiling that doesn't have any support or fixtures that could withstand the weight of a human.

The haunting of apartment 1610 seems to be a good late night ghost story for some students. It's said that a ghostly presence haunts the apartment's occupants. Some students have awakened to a dark shadow standing at the end of their bed. Others have observed the same dark shadow standing in the living room. Some students have even heard voices and footsteps come from unoccupied rooms. Students experiencing the paranormal activity offer their own conclusions to the haunting. Some believe it's the ghost of a former student who passed away but has his after-life home in a place he loved. Others suggest the ghost is a past student who was terminated from the program and has some unfinished business remaining. As time passes, it seems that the apartment number changes and so, too, does the content of the story. The ghost story is a tale that resurfaces each year.

It's said that a time capsule from 1996 is buried somewhere on property. The time capsule was put together by a group of students during their stay at Vista Way. Included in the time capsule are souvenirs from the Walt Disney World Resort's 25th anniversary celebration and Vista Way memorabilia such as identification cards, stories, program tips, secrets, photos, and even a special group photo of a select few Vista Way girls. Some have said the time capsule might be buried underneath either the volleyball court or under a marked tree somewhere on Vista Way property. A few students have attempted a small-scale search of the time capsule but have come up empty. Until a full-scale search is conducted, the time capsule will remain a mystery as to where it might be located, if one does really exist.

According to some students, a small treasure chest is buried somewhere on property. As the legend goes, a group of students in the late 1990's got together and gathered over $1,500 in donations from fellow students, friends, and family. The purpose was to create a scholarship fund for students having financial hardships while participating in the program. The group decided it would be more adventurous if they placed the money in a small chest and buried it somewhere on property. It's unknown if any students have claimed the so-called small fortune.

After opening the door to his apartment, a Fall, 1995 student discovered the unthinkable. An alligator had made its way into the apartment. Adding to the strange incident, the apartment was located on the third floor. After contacting housing security, the proper actions were taken. In a similar incident in spring, 2001, another alligator made its way into a third floor apartment. The legend has students telling the story with the same premise-a student coming home to the third floor apartment which is occupied by the green visitor.

The Vista Way Strip Club, located in one of the apartments, seems to popularize every now and then. According to students, the strip club was operational in the early 1990's. Female students looking to earn some extra money would entertain the male students. Even though the myth circulates each year, there is no proof of a Vista Way strip club ever existing.

In the late 1990's, two International female students believed prostitution was an easy way of making some extra money. Their operation was a success until two managers from the Walt Disney World Resort signed up for their services. Both the students and managers were caught and terminated. The Walt Disney Company denies such an act took place but students firmly believe the opposite. The legend is expanded upon each year such as the number of participants to the different types of sexual acts the students performed. In 2003, some students added that a small group of top Disney executives from corporate headquarters visited the two prostitutes but there's no record or proof of this ever occurring.

Celebrities visit the Walt Disney World Resort each year, but one legend has a certain celebrity visiting Vista Way on various occasions. It's said that Paris Hilton makes frequent visits to the apartment complex to party and take in the Disney College Program's environment.

Since the opening of Vista Way, many students come up with the belief that The Walt Disney Company will be issuing them a refund for rent that they've paid. Some say the company receives a tax break for students and charging rent is against the law. Others suggest that companies such as Coca-Cola or Microsoft purchased the apartment complexes and will be issuing the students a refund. During one year, students believed Michael Eisner's wife, Jane Eisner, purchased the apartment complexes and would be issuing them a refund. There's no record of Jane Eisner ever purchasing the Vista Way property. This is one myth that tends to grow and expand with new additions each year.

~

With the addition of Patterson Court within the vicinity of The Commons and Chatham Square, some may argue that over time these three complexes will eventually become the new Vista Way. Known for their calm and reserved environments, The Commons, Chatham Square, and Patterson Court still have their share of parties and craziness. As time passes it'll be interesting to see if this area truly becomes the 21st century version of Vista Way.

No matter what happens, the *Living* experience is so memorable and powerful that it's difficult to explain the impact it has on most students' lives. Shy students quickly turn the opposite as sociable students teach them the way of living life to its fullest extent. Students who participate in the program for a second or third term quickly learn an important lesson-the *Living* experience is never the same as their first program because roommates are different people who provide different emotions, hardships, and triumphs.

A Fall, 2003 alumna best describes the Living experience as the following: "You make each other laugh, listen to each other's problems and be there when the other is hurt. You talk with each other at 4:00 A.M. and nobody sleeps until everyone shuts up. Together, you clean the apartment, cook and make a mess of the dishes. The beer supply never runs out and the buffet of sex is endless. There's never a dull moment except for when trying to figure out which microwave dinner is the best to eat. The toughest decisions you have to make are either which party to attend or which guy or girl to 'hook up' with."

Chapter Six

LEARNING

We've got to fight against bigness. If a school gets too large, you lose an intimacy with the students; they begin to feel they're just part of a big complex. I don't think you can create too well in a big plant. That's why I always tried to avoid bigness in the studio...
—Walt Disney

Ever heard of a *Ducktorate* or a *Mousters*? No, these two words aren't incorrectly spelled. These are the two degrees offered during the Disney College Program if students choose to participate in the official *Learning* experience. A *Ducktorate* is awarded to students successfully completing a minimum of one of the Disney College Program Education courses, which are recommended for credit by the American Council on Education. A *Mousters* is awarded to students successfully completing a minimum of forty hours of approved Disney learning activities. For those students who wish not to participate in program coursework, they'll receive only a *Certificate of Completion*.

There are a variety of education courses offered to students. Students may enroll in two classes per program, fall or spring, at no cost. Most students take advantage of the free opportunity, even if they only take one course. Students are required to purchase their books and any other materials required for the courses they take.

The Disney Corporate Communications course explores and examines several areas including interpersonal communication, presentation skills, and complex situational topics such as meetings and facilitated classes. The course is equivalent to an Introductory Communications course.

A Spring, 2003 alumnus recalls: "The Communications course was the most basic course I'd ever taken. Being a Communications major, I could have taught the course. The course is beneficial to those early in their major. I slept three of the four hours at the back table and still got a ninety-seven percent in the class."

~

The Disney Marketing You course is a personal and career development strategies course designed to help students learn the basics of professionalism. Key elements of the course include the development of a career focus and a marketing plan. The marketing plan requires students to develop a commercial, cover letter, resume, and networking strategy. Students also learn interviewing and negotiation techniques. The course is designed for those who don't have experience on how to write a resume, cover letter, or prepare for the interview process. Generally, the course fills up with eighteen year old students who want to improve their skills for the professional world. Of all the courses offered, Marketing You is probably the least demanding and easiest way to earn the *Ducktorate* degree.

A College Program Education course professor recalls: "I couldn't believe how many students were unable to prepare a resume and cover letter. One student submitted a resume with his name incorrectly spelled. I gave it back to him and he turned in the resume, but his last name was incorrectly spelled. All I could do was scratch my head and wonder how he was even let into the program."

~

The Disney Experiential Learning course allows students to spend time at the beginning of the course studying theories on adult education and experiential learning. Several projects are completed outside of the classroom and in the *Learning Laboratory* of the Walt Disney World Resort. Students get the opportunity to explore the theme parks and apply their classroom knowledge to real world applications. Topics of diversity, community volunteering, and career exploration are a few of the topics discussed.

A Fall, 2000 alumna explains: "The Disney Experiential course is a definite course to take because you get to apply the learning material with a 'hands on' approach. The course is a nice supplement to the overall program."

~

The Disney Advanced Hospitality Management course focuses on the fundamental skills and knowledge needed in all areas of the hospitality and service industries. Students learn of what exceptional customer service consists, product knowledge, sales techniques, continuous improvement ethics, leadership, human resources, and financial matters in disciplines such as guest services, food and beverage, and merchandise. The course provides a solid foundation for students wishing to pursue a career in the hospitality industry.

A Fall, 2003 alumna states: "The course helped me get into a management position with Hilton Hotels. Disney is the best company to teach a Hospitality Management course."

~

The Disney Human Resource Management course is probably the most monotonous and slowest paced course offered. The course is designed to familiarize students with the current human resource practices and related laws. Students explore the human resource function in a corporate setting, specifically focusing on the development of knowledge and skills that most corporate managers need. Areas of study include employment law, labor relations, compensation, interviewing performance appraisal, training, and maintaining effective environments.

A Fall, 2003 alumnus recalls: "The Human Resources Management course was a nightmare. The course began at 8:00 A.M. and went right up 'til noon. The professor was boring and anal. I didn't learn a thing and didn't want to. The only thing I got out of the class was a threesome late one night with the girls who sat at my table. So, yeah, it was human management in some ways."

~

The Disney Corporate Analysis course is a newer addition to the *Learning* experience. The course focuses on The Walt Disney Company, its success at productivity, and how the company values culture and diversity. The company's history is explored as well as how the organization thrives on being innovative and technological.

A Fall, 2009 alumnus states: "This is a solid foundational course that provides students with corporate philosophies and other corporate jargon. The course covers everything from a financial perspective to a creative outlook. There's a nice and beneficial balance."

~

A Disney Creativity & Innovation course is also a new addition to the *Learning* experience. The course utilizes successful theories on how to contribute to the creative team and how to manage creativity. It also helps students prepare for organizational demands without losing that creative spirit.

A Fall, 2009 alumnus states: "This is a good course for students who need a creative boost or have difficulty executing their creative ideas or talents. I highly recommend it."

~

A Disney Organizational Leadership course is offered to students and should be highly considered for any future leaders of America. The course can be best described as an Advanced Communications course in the program. The knowledge of leadership theory and how to apply it is a central theme in the course. Students examine and apply the classical models of leadership in preparation of their application in today's corporate environment. Throughout the course, students examine various aspects of leadership and re-examine the results of their own leadership styles. Although classes can be long and tedious at times, the professors attempt best to engage the entire class in discussion.

A Fall, 2003 alumnus remembers: "Our professor taught the course using a golf club. He swung that thing around, lectured with it and used it as a pointer. During one class, he almost took my eye out by mistake. It was hilarious and the class really was in tune with what he talked about. I suppose if you weren't, he'd take your eye out."

~

A professional development series is provided to students interested in major-specific areas. Engineering, entertainment, security and finance are all avenues for students to explore. Additional learning opportunities can be pursued as well. The educational component of the program strives to meet the needs of every student who wishes to take advantage of the beneficial opportunities.

A Fall, 2005 alumnus recalls: "I got the opportunity to work with a Disney marketing team and completed a marketing plan. I learned all of the fundamentals of creating and implementing a full-scale plan. I took the plan back to my university and was given two additional college units for the project. There are opportunities that cater to every student."

The Disney Exploration Series offers students the opportunity to take their established learning outcomes and experience Walt Disney World as never before. Students have the opportunity to explore the communication processes, guest service, leadership, marketing, and people management. Disney leaders speak to the students and demonstrate what works and what doesn't. Students have the opportunity to experience certain sessions out in the Walt Disney World Resort to obtain a complete perspective of the topic matter.

A Fall, 2009 alumna states: "Take advantage of this series because you get to network with Disney leaders and have the opportunity to help problem-solve selected issues in certain areas. There are no textbooks or exams required!"

~

Students have the opportunity to take advantage of additional *Learning* experiences while in the program. Students have access to Disney Learning Center Resources where books, magazines, CD's, and DVD's are available. Special course offerings provide students with the opportunity to listen to a Disney leader or to program alumni discuss topics that might include time management, leadership, and personal brand, just to name a few. These are just some of the additional *Learning* experiences offered, but it's very apparent that Disney wants students to learn all they can while in the program. Where else can students receive a first-class developmental experience that is free? In the real world, business professionals would have to pay thousands of dollars for one session. Don't let this opportunity escape.

~

Disney College Program Education courses are similar to traditional university courses. There are guidelines for students to follow, and failure to comply results in failure of the course. One of these guidelines is that students must wear business casual clothing and nametags at all times. Students aren't allowed to drag themselves into an 8:00 A.M. class wearing only pajamas. No matter how professionally dressed students might be, wardrobe malfunctions do frequently occur.

During one group presentation, a female student was in the middle of actively discussing leadership theories by jumping up and down and all around in the front of the room. Suddenly, her left breast flew out of her shirt and gave the entire class a little extra in her presentation. It's unknown as to what grade the female student received.

Prior to one afternoon class, a routine thunderstorm occurred as students entered the classroom. A busty female wearing a soaked white t-shirt walked into the classroom, and the male students quickly discovered she wasn't wearing a bra. The male professor had a very difficult time lecturing for the first hour of the class on that particular day.

Walking up to give his presentation for one class, the pants of a male student surprisingly fell down below his knees. The bigger surprise was the pink thong he was wearing. He quickly pulled up his pants and provided an "A" presentation.

A Fall, 1999 alumna explains: "Disney might as well have marched us into the room and shackled our legs to the tables. I was asked to leave a class because I wasn't wearing my nametag. The nametags should have included barcodes for the Professors or security guards to scan."

A Spring, 2000 alumnus remembers: "I didn't have a belt for my slacks, which were a bit loose. I used a black rope from my truck. As I was leaving class the professor called me over. He gave me $20, so I could buy a black belt."

A Spring, 2005 alumnus describes the courses as: "Show off your wardrobe, look good for the opposite sex and hope to 'get some' later that night. Nametags required, however."

~

A number of students typically show up for their class, sign-in, and then leave the class. Students are also notorious for signing-in their friends who are most likely at home recovering from a hangover. One student signed two of her friends' names on the roll sheet. Without realizing that she was the only student sitting at the table, the roll sheet was given to the professor.

Later in the class, the professor approached the incompetent student and informed her how kind and thoughtful she was to think of her two friends. The professor failed her and her two friends for the class in which she and all of her friends had well above a passing grade before the incident.

Attendance is required for successful completion of a course, and students may only miss two class meetings. Students aren't required to notify their professor if they miss a class but some don't understand this concept.

A Spring, 1998 alumnus recalls: "I called the professor to inform him I was sick and going to miss class. He thanked me for calling and suddenly the Magic Kingdom opening announcement came across the loud speaker in the background. All I could do was hang up and hope he wouldn't figure it out. At the next class meeting, the professor suggested that the next time I call-in sick I do it from home, in bed and not at the theme park."

A Fall, 2000 alumnus remembers: "I couldn't miss anymore classes, so I called my professor and told her that I caught a sexually transmitted disease the night before. The professor believed me, and two weeks later I actually caught a sexually transmitted disease. This time, however, she didn't believe me."

A Fall, 2003 alumna recalls: "I called my professor and told her the truth. I was unable to make the class because I was hung over."

A Spring, 2004 alumnus remembers: "I had missed two classes already and was hung over. I couldn't make it to class, so I told my professor that my grandmother died, which she hadn't. A month later my family came to visit, including my grandmother. We ran into my professor at the park and I was frantic. At the next class meeting the professor asked how my grandmother was recovering from her death. I turned a bit red but the professor let it slide."

~

The grading system is Pass/Fail, with passing being seventy percent or higher. Even though the courses are free, assignments are still required to be turned in before the appropriate deadlines for passing grades.

A Fall, 1998 alumna remembers: "My assignments were always weeks late and I still got a ninety-five percent in the class. I just bought my professor all the beers he wanted at Pleasure Island and I had all the time I needed to complete my assignments. I owned him and I think he knew it."

A Fall, 2001 alumnus recalls: "I turned a paper in one hour after the class concluded. The professor took the paper and without hesitation marked an 'F' on it."

A Spring, 2002 alumnus remembers: "I couldn't turn my paper in on time because the night before, my roommate had sex with a girl. Let's just say he used the paper to wipe up after himself."

~

In-class behavior shouldn't have to be stressed in college level courses, but the College Program is a completely different world. Students are expected to participate, to actively listen, and to stay awake. Sleeping in class is a constant problem because students party the night before and are exhausted for their four hour class. Some students choose to sit in the back

148

where they try their best to stay out-of-view from the professor. During a long lecture, one student placed his head down on the table and began snoring as the professor lectured the class. The snoring became louder until the professor startled the student out of his deep sleep.

In a separate incident, one tired student fell asleep with his head down on the table. The professor continued with his lecture until the student began screaming from a nightmare.

Afternoon classes can be tough for students to remain awake, and for one exhausted student such was the case. As the class concluded, the sleeping student didn't move a muscle. The room cleared out, and the professor decided to leave the tired student sleeping. Two hours later, the student woke up to an empty classroom.

Another student was so tired that he signed the roll sheet and crawled under the table to sleep during the entire class. At the end of the class, he woke up, signed the second required roll sheet, and left the classroom.

Other students have found creative ways to sleep during their four hour class. During one student's 8:00 A.M. class, he sneaked into the classroom's closet during the class' first break. He closed the door and went to sleep. The student woke up and exited the closet not knowing it was 3:00 P.M. A second class was taking place in the room, and the student walked right past the professor giving a lecture, excused himself, and exited the room.

Even though some students may not consider the Disney College Program Education courses equivalent to university courses, the message is made clear every year; if a student cheats, he or she will be expelled from the course and possibly terminated from the program. One student learned the hard way as he went on-line and printed out an essay to submit. The suspicious professor asked the student from which web site the essay was retrieved, and the student denied the accusation. The professor explained that a former student had turned in the exact same essay a few years back. The student was kicked out of the class.

A Fall, 2002 alumna recalls: "We were taking a test and I looked over at my friend's paper for an answer. I got the answer, wrote it on my paper and looked up. Standing there looking at me was the professor and I failed the course. The answers I copied from my friend weren't even the correct answers."

~

In the early 1990's, pagers were a problem in the classroom. Today, the problem has become the use of cell phones. Students often forget to turn their cell phones off, while some students don't understand that answering a cell phone in the middle of a lecture is disrespectful. Perhaps professors should collect students' cell phones at the door before classes begin as many students are unable to be away from their phones for a few hours.

A Fall, 2002 alumnus recalls: "I sat in the front and my cell phone rang while it was on the table. The professor walked over, grabbed the phone and answered it. She told them to call me back and explained why I should turn my cell phone off during class. I was bright red to say the least."

A Spring, 2003 alumnus remembers: "My phone rang during class and I answered it as the professor was lecturing. He stopped his lecture as I continued talking with my friend about how drunk we got the night before. I made plans to go drinking for the upcoming weekend and everything. Five minutes later the conversation concluded and the professor resumed. I think everyone in the class couldn't believe what just happened."

~

After successful completion of the course with a passing grade of seventy percent or higher, students receive that prized *Ducktorate*. Many students take a course just for the degree. After all, how many people have the honor of holding a *Ducktorate* degree? Most students who hold a *Mousters* or *Ducktorate* are proud to have earned such a degree. The degree on a resume makes for great conversation starters in interviews due to the uniqueness of the degree. Past students have been offered positions because the degree on their resume and conversations about the degree provided a unique difference from other candidates.

One student earned four *Ducktorates* and one *Mousters* during a one-year period. After obtaining the degrees, the student went home and applied at a Computer Software Company. The only other qualification the student had was an Associate of Science degree from his local community college. The student was offered a six-figure income with his new job and later learned it was the *Ducktorate* and *Mousters* that made the difference. The company appreciated the creativity along with the skills, which the degrees provided the student.

A Fall, 2003 alumna states: "The degree really doesn't do anything for your resume with the exception of raising questions that you don't know how to spell the word Doctorate."

A Fall, 2004 alumna states: "I had my Mousters professionally framed!"

A Fall, 2004 alumnus remembers an interview: "The interviewer asked me why I misspelled Doctorate. I tried explaining what a Ducktorate was and he laughed at me. He asked if I was certified to quack."

A Spring, 2005 alumnus recalls an interview: "I was asked if I earned my bachelor's degree. I said, 'No, but I have my Mouster's degree.' The interviewer said that was even better. I think he thought I said 'Master's,' but I wasn't going to argue with him. I was offered the position and I accepted."

~

Networking is an essential component of the *Learning* experience. According to Walt Disney World Resort leadership, a majority of students in the program fail to network because they lack a proactive approach. Program recruiters, managers, and other personnel encourage the importance of networking during a student's stay in the program. Students who network are at an advantage in climbing up the Disney corporate ladder.

A Fall, 2002 alumna recalls: "I networked with everyone possible and met with Disney leaders. Two weeks after my program concluded, I was offered a Guest Service Manager role. I believe my networking abilities increased my chances."

A Guest Service Manager from the Magic Kingdom states: "I remember the students who take the initiative in learning and meeting with my team and other management personnel. Those are the students who we turn to when a leadership role needs to be filled. We look for personality, determination, team building skills, and superior guest service abilities."

~

LEARNING

The combination of taking a Disney College Program Education course and networking with other cast members greatly enhances the overall experience and value of the College Program. Disney continually improves and changes the necessary components of the *Learning* experience. Courses are improved upon and changed over time to meet the real world's intellectual demands. Networking opportunities and self-improvement seminars are provided to those interested in improving their skills. Even though students obtain many *Learning* experiences outside of the classroom, taking a course that is full of useful information is an effective supplement.

Chapter Seven

ESCAPE

Fantasy and reality often overlap.
—Walt Disney

Long weeks at work combined with education courses make it difficult for students to escape Disney property. Exploring outside of the Walt Disney World Resort is a large part of the College Program experience. When students get the opportunity to break free from the program for a day or two, they do so in full force. There are plenty of experiences for students to explore in the Orlando area, or *O-Town*, as most students refer to it. From the sandy beaches to the area nightclubs, energetic students invade the Orlando area on a regular basis.

~

Half a block from Vista Way is Walgreens Drugstore. For quick and convenient purchases, students routinely shop there because of the short walk. The store is also conveniently situated for students without automobiles. The drugstore is host to unique shopping experiences for several students. One desperate student attempted to make his purchase with *Disney Dollars*, a currency only acceptable at Disney theme parks. When the cashier declined the currency, the student remarked, "No problem. I stole the money from Disney anyway."

During one midnight visit, a student decided not to pay for a bottle of Jack Daniels. He took the bottle and drank most of it while sitting on the floor in a store aisle. After finishing the bottle, the student walked out and went on his way.

Some students need to be reminded that sports-related activities should take place outside of the store. Two students decided to use a store aisle to bowl. The deodorant sticks acted as pins, and a small container of face cream was used as the bowling ball.

In a separate sporting event, two students began playing catch with a miniature football inside the store. While throwing the football back and forth between aisles three and seven, a pass came up short and smacked a little old lady in the face on aisle six.

Three other students thought it was a good idea to race shopping carts down three separate aisles. As the winner of the race crossed the finish line, he forgot to stop and ran the shopping cart right into the allergy medication shelf. The student quickly ran out of the store and never returned.

A former Walgreen's Drugstore employee remembers: "The Disney College Program students came in on a regular basis. They were all a good group of kids who made our jobs a lot more enjoyable. Late one night, a male student came into the store wearing only a thong and flip flops."

A former Walgreen's Drugstore employee recalls: "The top two items I sold to students on a constant basis were hard liquor and condoms. One student asked if we carried any Disney themed condoms."

~

Wendy's fast food restaurant is located next door to Vista Way. The restaurant is so close to the housing complex that students can hop the wall and immediately be at the front door. The layout of the apartment complex, however, doesn't allow this easy access. Students must walk clear around and over to the security checkpoint to leave the property. One brave student believed climbing the wall would be a quicker route to Wendy's. Midway through his climb, security caught the student and issued him a warning.

In a separate climbing attempt, five students decided to make a midnight food run to Wendy's. One student, however, decided climbing the wall would be faster as the other four students chose to drive. The climber got stuck on the wall and couldn't get down. A few minutes later, the climber's four friends drove by, food and all, as he was being questioned by security. The student said, "I thought we were allowed to climb the walls."

Once students actually make it inside the restaurant, some normal patrons get to experience College Program students at their best. During one late night dinner, several students decided to have a chicken nugget fight. After a large number of nuggets flew across the restaurant, local police officials were called-in to break up the food fight.

One intoxicated student needed to use the restaurant's bathroom. After twenty minutes, employees discovered the entire bathroom had been covered in protein spill. The wall, stall, sink, and floor were all from one student.

In a separate incident, a male student quickly went into the bathroom to vomit. With his head in the toilet bowl, two women walked in. To the student's surprise and embarrassment, he had entered the women's bathroom by mistake.

During a visit to the drive-thru, one student drove past the service window, stopped and reversed back to the window. Forgetting his automobile was still in the reverse gear, the student accelerated and crashed into the vehicle behind him. Surprisingly, the driver of the other vehicle was his girlfriend.

A Fall, 2002 alumna recalls: "After a late night and a lot of alcohol at Pleasure Island, we'd use the Wendy's bathroom if we couldn't make it to our apartment in time."

A Fall, 2005 alumna remembers: "I ordered my food, pulled up to the drive-thru window, paid and drove away without collecting my food. I quickly realized what I did and pulled around to the window a second time to get my food. I was in a hurry to get to a party at Vista Way."

~

Students find it most convenient to conduct all of their shopping at the local Wal-Mart. Wal-Mart is also a stop on the program bus route for those who don't have an automobile. Students normally need to shop well after midnight due to late night shifts, so the twenty-four hour Super-Center is the perfect choice.

No matter what time students shop at Wal-Mart, store employees have the honor of serving some of the finest and brightest college students in the country. One clever student asked a store employee if they sold blinker fluid for her automobile. More surprisingly, the store employee told the student they were all out and would be having a selection of blinker fluid on sale the following week.

As a prank, one student asked his roommate to call the store requesting fat-free lard. The roommate made the call, and after thirty minutes of waiting on-hold, the student realized there was no such thing as fat-free lard.

During a midnight shopping spree, five roommates purchased $300 worth of groceries and apartment supplies. After the items were scanned and the amount was requested, the students realized that not one of them had their wallets.

Another student purchased over $100 worth of groceries and while approaching his car, his cell phone suddenly rang. The student answered his cell phone, began talking, got into his car and drove away, leaving his groceries behind. When he realized what had just occurred, the student made a quick u-turn and drove back to the parking lot. Luckily for him, a Wal-Mart associate had just retrieved the cart of groceries.

One unlucky student went shopping at 3:00 A.M., after a closing shift at the Magic Kingdom. The student paid and went out to his car, only to discover that his car had been stolen. A few hours later, police officials located the stolen car and suspect. The victim's roommate had stolen his car. The car was recovered, and the thief was terminated from the program.

A Fall, 2003 alumna recalls: "I shopped at Wal-Mart because it was open all the time and was the cheapest. Since we weren't paid much, we had no choice."

A Spring, 2004 alumnus remembers: "We needed a place to shop at in the middle of the night since we worked at the Magic Kingdom. If it wasn't for Wal-Mart, a lot of students would have never been able to shop."

ESCAPE

A Fall, 2005 alumna states: "Before being in the College Program you don't appreciate Wal-Mart. During the program, you quickly learn to appreciate Wal-Mart's convenience, prices and variety."

Another Fall, 2005 alumna remembers: "Pleasure Island, the beach and Wal-Mart were the most visited locations during my time in the program. Wal-Mart was the only place to shop at in the middle of the night."

~

Some of the more popular hangouts for students in the Orlando area are the bars. Students and cast members live the night away celebrating yet another day survived in the Mouse House, and the last topic discussed is Disney.

The Ale House is one of the more popular bars students visit. Close distance and excellent prices attract many after-hours students and fellow co-workers. Other popular hangouts in the past have included Cheers, Bennigan's, Jelly Rolls, Big Bamboo, Bahama Breeze, Taboo, Kitty O' Sheas, and Jungle Jim's. From happy hours and $1 drinks to karaoke, all locations have something to offer for each student.

Some students become so intoxicated that they have trouble controlling their actions. One student was so drunk during her karaoke session at Cheers, she began singing out the names of every guy she had sex with during her time in the program, including two of her managers from work.

One brave student began dancing on a table at Jungle Jim's during a friendly gathering. What appeared to be a normal dance evolved into something shocking as she began stripping off her clothing. Even more surprising was that her parents showed up for what was to be a surprise birthday party for her.

A rather talented student was doing the Hokey Pokey onstage at Jelly Rolls when he suddenly tripped and fell flat on his face. For his remaining time in the program, he was better known as "Pokey."

There are times when students' managers from work like to crash the parties, but most students prevent such occurrences. One student called-in sick and went to Cheers for a Friday night Halloween party. The female student was dressed up in a costume, and an older guy began flirting with her. She realized it was her manager from work and quickly left the bar.

During a round of beers, two students at Bennigan's were bashing their manager from work when the guy at the table next to them asked the students to keep the conversation quieter. To the students' surprise, the angry guy was none other than their manager listening to the entire session of himself being bashed. No action was taken, and no hostile environment was created for the students at work.

A Fall, 2003 alumna states: "It's very common that students and their managers go out with each other to get hammered. My manager and I got so drunk one night that his wife had to come and pick us up. I actually vomited all over her car floor on the ride home."

A Fall, 2005 alumna recalls: "One of our managers would go out to the local bars and try 'picking up' drunk CP girls. To my knowledge, he was turned down one hundred percent of the time."

~

After a night of partying students generally become very hungry at 2:00 A.M. Few places remain open twenty-four hours and one of those places that does is Steak n' Shake. A famous steak burger or thick and creamy milkshake meets the demands of any starving student early in the morning. Some visits provide magical morning moments that only a College Program student could make happen. During one early morning visit, a hungry student decided hamburgers and milkshakes weren't enough to fill his appetite. After consuming two coloring crayons, his appetite was finally satisfied.

A Fall, 2003 alumnus recalls: "We'd just carry the party on over to Steak n' Shake. We were there until daylight and left after we had breakfast."

A Fall, 2004 alumna remembers: "We got a little crazy and I remember seeing one guy flop down on a table. I don't think the guy had a single drink that night. We were all having a great time."

A Fall, 2007 alumnus remembers: "We worked at Magic Kingdom and were there at midnight when we got into a fight with a crew from Epcot. A few punches were thrown and when it was all said and done we were all sitting at the same table. Not quite sure what even started the fight."

~

The success of the Walt Disney World Resort cleared the way for other theme park destinations in the Orlando area. Sea World, Universal Studios Orlando, and Tampa Bay's Busch Gardens are all popular attractions for students to visit. During a Universal Studios *Halloween Horror Nights* event, a group of male students decided it would be a clever idea to leave their female friend behind in one of the haunted houses. Frightened, the female student remained lost until she met one of the employees playing a gruesome monster as part of the haunted house. One year later, the two got married. A bad situation turned into a happy ending.

A Fall, 2005 alumna states: "It's nice to see what other theme parks have to offer. You see how nice the Disney parks really are."

~

The top destinations for students to visit off property are the local beaches. After students contact their work location with excuses for missing work, they load up their automobiles and head out to invade Cocoa Beach and Daytona Beach.

Resisting a daily visit to the beach is difficult for most students, and sometimes their only option to make such a visit is calling-in excuses to work or leaving work early. One student called his boss and informed him that he couldn't make it to work because his car broke down. In reality, his car was stuck on the sand of Daytona Beach and would remain stuck for the remainder of the day.

Three students skipped work so they could visit Cocoa Beach. One of the students called his manager and explained he had the flu. Later in the day, the sick student ran into his manager at the beach. Apparently, the student's manager had to go home sick as well.

In a separate incident, one student had a 4:00 P.M. work shift and decided to make a quick visit to Daytona Beach. The student took a nap on the beach and woke up a few hours later, only to discover the time was 6:00 P.M. The student hurried back to Lake Buena Vista and was hours late for his shift.

Some students experience the beaches for their first time. One confused student who made her first visit to the ocean asked her roommate what chemical Florida used to keep the water so blue.

Another student was hesitant to get into the water at Daytona Beach and asked her boyfriend if there were alligators in the ocean. Her boyfriend explained there were no alligators, only sharks. The hesitant student quickly got into the water and was not concerned with the possibility of nearby sharks.

Visits to the beach also cause unusual incidents among students. Two students made a friendly wager on how far they could drive their jeep into the waters of Daytona Beach. The over-confident students drove out into the water, only to get their jeep stuck until local authorities could show up to assist.

During one busy weekday afternoon, three students were tossing a frisbee on Daytona Beach when a small fight suddenly broke out a few feet away. About thirty minutes later, the three students learned that their manager from work had caused the riot. The manager ended up with two black eyes and the students ended up with some leverage. For the remainder of their program, the students' manager granted most of their work-related requests.

A Spring, 2001 alumnus states: "Four years after my program, my car still has sand in it from Daytona Beach."

A Fall, 2004 alumnus recalls: "We arrived at Daytona Beach and I ran straight into the water without thinking. I ruined my cell phone, soaked my wallet and lost my money. I had never seen the ocean before, so I was excited."

A Spring, 2005 alumna states: "A lot of College Program students have never seen the ocean or even a beach, so Daytona Beach or Cocoa Beach is quite a sight for them."

~

Participation in the College Program gives students the benefit of free theme park admission to all Walt Disney World Resort theme parks. When students don't escape Disney property to explore the local non-Disney attractions, they head for the Disney theme parks. Calling-in sick and going to a Disney theme park on the same day isn't the smartest move. Once a student scans his or her card at the theme park's main entrance, the name of that student is registered into the computer. Being in the computer system as a call-in and as a guest in the park on the same day is bad news for anyone who attempts the risk. This can be easily tracked by managers if they choose to do so.

Some students don't take the call-in policy seriously and quickly learn that cheating the Mouse will result in severe consequences; well, maybe not that severe. One brilliant student called-in sick and went to the Magic Kingdom. However, his role while in the program was Park Greeter at the Magic Kingdom's main entrance. The not-so-clever student should have at least visited one of the other three theme parks because the student's manager caught him before he even made it through the turnstile. The student was given a warning, and he didn't make that mistake again, at least not at the Magic Kingdom.

During two students' visit to Epcot, security and their manager approached the two students at the main entrance. Both students worked at Epcot and both called-in sick at the same time with the same excuse. The students' manager gave them a warning and explained that the next time they called-in sick, they should visit another theme park.

After another clever student called-in sick for two straight days, he returned to work and his manager asked, "How are you feeling? How was Epcot? How was the Magic Kingdom?" The shocked student was speechless that his manager knew of his recent visits to the theme parks. It turned out that the student went through the turnstiles instead of entering the park through a backstage area.

A Fall, 2003 alumna states: "You can call-in sick and still go to the parks. You just have to go through a backstage entrance and sneak out onstage. Don't go through the turnstile!"

A Spring, 2005 alumna remembers: "I worked at the Magic Kingdom and called-in sick one morning. I went to the Magic Kingdom later in the day and entered through a backstage area. I walked around a corner while onstage and ran right into my manager. He just asked how I was, and we both went our separate ways."

~

Students who play in the Disney theme parks during their days off take full advantage. They normally have a favorite theme park, and if they work at a theme park while in the program, chances are that is the least favorite one for them to visit. Every Thursday is payday for Walt Disney World Resort cast members, but for students, the real meaning of Thursday used to be free admission to Pleasure Island. Students would take advantage of the free admission and party until 2:00 AM.

A Fall, 2003 alumna recalls: "They had a Magic Kingdom welcoming party for CP's. We got to ride Space Mountain with the lights on. It's creepier than with the lights out because you can see how close you are to the tracks. After riding it with the lights on, I definitely stopped riding the attraction with my hands in the air."

A Spring, 2004 alumnus recalls: "Every Thursday we'd see all of our friends and co-workers drinking and dancing at Pleasure Island. One night, I was on the dance floor at the BET Soundstage Club and bumped into my manager from work. Disney cast members ruled Thursday nights at Pleasure Island."

A Fall, 2004 alumna remembers: "We'd do the 'Wishes' dance while watching the 'Wishes' fireworks spectacular at the Magic Kingdom. People looked at us like we were nuts. We just told them we were CP's."

A Fall, 2005 alumna states: "Free admission to the theme parks is a huge perk!"

A Spring, 2006 alumnus remembers: "We were in the Beach Club, and I didn't have a single drink. I vomited all over the bathroom floor, and it just kept coming out. The irony is that I'm probably the only guy to get that sick in a club without even having one drink."

~

Golf fanatics are in paradise at the Walt Disney World Resort. Whether it's an eighteen-hole PGA course or a miniature golf course, students interested in golf have several options. During an afternoon golf game, a student lost his ball in a water hazard. Determined to get his ball back, the student went into the water. His friend began yelling "alligator" as the reptile approached the student trying to grab his ball. The student saw he had a visitor and quickly vacated the area.

In a separate incident, two students approached their golf cart and discovered they had a friendly visitor. An alligator was guarding their golf cart, and the two decided that walking back to the clubhouse would be the safer alternative.

166

Miniature golf can be as equally challenging as a pro golf course, and some students become frustrated with their miniature abilities. While playing a round of miniature golf with a group of friends, an overly aggressive student hit his ball as far as he could. After the game the group approached the parking lot and discovered that the ball was hit through the student's car windshield.

In a separate incident, another student was frustrated with his miniature golf score and threw his putter across the course. The putter smacked a nearby guest in the face, and the student quickly learned that the victim was none other than his girlfriend. The unlucky girlfriend required four stitches for her injury.

During an evening miniature golf game, a student became so frustrated with his poor score that he took his anger out on a snowman's head and arms. The snowman's arm was knocked into a nearby fountain, and the other arm landed in front of a young guest.

One student lacking in skills was on his hands and knees looking for his lost blue ball in the bushes. When asked by a nearby player if everything was okay, the student responded, "Yep, just looking for my blue balls."

A Spring, 2005 alumnus recalls: "My golf clubs were stolen out of my car while I was at work one day. About one month after I returned home, I discovered my golf clubs being sold on EBay. I looked a little closer and realized the person selling my golf clubs was one of my managers from work."

~

Traveling on Florida freeways and highways can be a bit challenging for many tourists and a troublesome pain for students. SR535 and I-4 are the two main routes that lead into and out of Walt Disney World Resort property. One rebellious student routinely used the shoulder to pass lost and confused tourists. One night, however, Disney security ended the student's alternate route by giving him a traffic citation. The student said, "But I'm a CP!"

One student believed he was smarter than the toll crossings as he'd toss buttons into the collection bowl. This is one of the oldest tricks in the book, but the student opened his mail one afternoon and learned the trick was on him. He received a bill for over $300.

On her first day of work, a lost student drove around in circles on Walt Disney World Resort property looking for the Magic Kingdom cast member parking lot. She drove out of her circle and ended up at Sea World, miles away from where she was supposed to be.

Unfortunately for most students, resort guests also drive on Walt Disney World Resort property. While driving to work one day, a student got a flat tire on I-4. As he changed the tire, a tourist pulled over to ask where he could find I-5. The perplexed student thought about it for a moment and realized I-5 was in California. He explained the differences between I-4 and I-5 to the tourist. Confused, the tourist asked which exit would take him to I-5. The student gave up and informed the guest to look for the "California Exit" a few miles west.

In a separate incident, a tourist flagged down two students on Walt Disney World Resort property and asked where the Walt Disney World Resort was located. The students explained he was at the Walt Disney World Resort. In disbelief, the confused tourist continued asking. The helpful students directed the tourist to Universal Studios Orlando instead. One of the students said, "Now remember, if you end up in Atlanta, Georgia, you've gone too far!"

A Fall, 2003 alumnus states: "After tourists drive under the Walt Disney World Resort sign, a laser zaps their brains and sucks all common sense out of them."

A Fall, 2004 alumnus recalls: "I was at a stop light and the driver in the car next to me asked where Epcot was located. I pointed to the sign in front of us that stated, 'Epcot: Next Left.' The driver asked if he was to turn left or right."

A Spring, 2006 alumna remembers: "I was stopped at the Epcot Toll Plaza and a driver rear-ended my vehicle. I got out of the car and the only thing the driver could ask was where Walt Disney World was located. I explained that he was on Walt Disney World property and he said, 'No, not this one. The bigger Walt Disney World.' I interrupted and reminded him what just happened and he said, 'Oh, not a problem. I don't have insurance.' "

~

There are educational attractions to explore in Florida as well. Students routinely make their way to Kennedy Space Center for the Space Shuttle launches. Students either take a day off from work or visit the center a day or two after their program concludes. College Program personnel encourage students to attend a Space Shuttle launch as it's an amazing sight to see and experience.

On the morning of January 25, 1986, three students called-in sick and traveled to Kennedy Space Center. Expecting a fun and exciting morning of watching one of America's greatest sights, the unexpected occurred. Seventy-three seconds into the mission, the Space Shuttle Challenger exploded right before the students' very own eyes.

One student recalls: "The entire nation was in shock. Our managers didn't care that we called-in sick so we could be there. The only thing our managers cared about was how we were handling what we just experienced in-person."

~

Give Kids the World Village is a seventy acre, nonprofit resort in Central Florida that creates magical memories for children with life-threatening illnesses and their families. Many College Program students help with Parents' Night Out, which is scheduled on selected nights. During Parents' Night Out, students visit the village and watch the children of Give Kids the World families so parents can go out for date night dinners at nearby restaurants. For most of these parents, an evening out alone is a rare and much appreciated treat. For some students, the experience is quite heart-warming and emotional. Students who participate in the program don't volunteer for school credit or for compensation; they volunteer solely to promote goodwill. Students who participate should be commended and applauded for their spirited efforts.

A Fall, 2003 alumnus recalls: "I had a good feeling that I was helping those kids. I got attached to them in just a few short hours."

A Fall, 2004 alumna remembers: "I met one of the kids' parents and they were very thankful for what we did. The mother said I made her daughter feel so special and the happiest she'd ever been."

A Spring, 2005 alumna recalls: "I told one kid that I was a friend of Mickey Mouse and Donald Duck. His eyes lit up and he was so excited that I knew Mickey and Donald."

ESCAPE

A Fall, 2005 alumnus states: "Every student should volunteer at least one time. You get to meet a lot of great kids."

~

Every student in the College Program has a favorite place in Florida outside of the world of Disney. Some like the local nightclubs and bars while others enjoy a relaxing day at Daytona Beach. Students utilizing their free theme park admission get to experience what would cost most people thousands of dollars. The adventures students explore outside of Disney and even on Disney property help them cope with the daily stresses of the *Living*, *Learning*, and *Earning* experiences. After all, the program is still a form of college, and not only is college supposed to be an educational experience, but also a fun one as well. The time quickly passes, and before all too long, the program does begin to conclude. For those who don't play and explore outside of the Walt Disney World Resort, regrets are imminent.

Chapter Eight

CHECKING-OUT

A good ending is vital to a picture, the single most important element, because it is what the audience takes with them out of the theater.
—Walt Disney

The sun begins to set on a journey that changes most students' lives. For many students, the time catches up with them and the end quickly nears. After living with the same people for several months and working with fellow cast members five to six days per week, the reality presents itself to every student; the time has come to return to the real world.

The last few days of a student's program tend to be full of anticipation of returning home but also full of hugs and tears from both the male and female students. It may take tremendous courage to leave home and participate in the program, but it takes greater courage to leave the program. Some students are terrified of returning to the real world they left months prior. As students finish up their last day of work and make final preparations in packing up their personal belongings, checking-out becomes more chaotic than a Disney theme park on a holiday.

Describing the reality of going home to non-program participants is difficult. One former student best describes the reality of leaving the program with the following statement, which was obtained from www.disneyalumni.com:

"When you spend this much time with people, you get really close. You are the only people around; no family, no friends from school, nobody. You all come down almost completely alone, or with other people from your school that you might not see much. You experience things together that no one back home will understand. They don't quite get the feeling of stepping out onto your apartment balcony at 9:00 P.M. to watch the Epcot fireworks every night, or the feeling of helping a guest and knowing that what you do creates lasting memories in their lives forever. You share the magic with thousands of people daily. The magic of Disney is something that will touch you in a way that nothing else ever will. And you share all of this with your roommates and fellow program students. You experience all of this, go through holidays together and become each other's family."

~

The last day at work can be quite emotional for students as they've become familiar with a daily routine consisting of fairy tale castles, large golf-ball shaped icons, larger than life fake trees, spinning teacups, and characters that each student grew up with through the years of watching television. Most can't wait until the nightmare of working for minimum wage concludes, but deep down, each student carries a love-it/hate-it attitude about the program.

A Spring, 1999 alumnus states: "You love the program, hate it and love it. The reality is that the program is something special for everyone who participates."

A Fall, 2001 alumnus remembers: "I left the program not wanting to think about Disney ever again. After two days at home, I realized how much I missed the program and the entire experience."

A Fall, 2002 alumna recalls: "On my last day of work it hit me that I wouldn't be walking down Main Street U.S.A. the next day. After six months of working in the fairy tale world, it was going to be different out in the 'real' world."

A Spring, 2009 alumnus states: "The program is special and I would have done it for free. You learn tough life lessons, responsibility, and professionalism."

~

Disney holds a graduation ceremony to commemorate students' accomplishments in the program. The ceremony celebrates the *Living*, *Learning* and *Earning* experiences. Guest speakers are invited to speak to students about their hard work, and plenty of refreshments are provided. Graduates are provided with graduation caps in the shape of Mickey Mouse ears. Mickey and Minnie Mouse even show up for the special day dressed in their finest graduation attire.

The graduation ceremony is a time to reflect and enjoy the friendships made during the program. Some students take the opportunity to do a little more. During one graduation ceremony, three students sneaked in their very own hard liquor for the celebration. As the guest speaker delivered his speech, the three students tried competing as to how many shots they could take before the speaker concluded his statements. The winner was able to handle eighteen shots. The student passed out in Epcot shortly after.

Another student fell asleep during an early morning ceremony and began snoring quite loudly during the guest speaker's presentation. A nearby student woke up the snoring student. Two minutes later the student fell back asleep and resumed snoring.

A Fall, 2003 alumnus states: "I took my mouse ears and used the cap for my college graduation. It really stood out."

A Spring, 2004 alumna states: "The graduation ceremony is a nice touch and it helps insert some of the 'fun' back into the program."

~

On most students' last day, they receive a written evaluation from their manager. The evaluation explains how well they performed during their *Earning* experience. Most evaluations are positive, but on rare occasions there are evaluations quite the opposite. One student's evaluation indicated he needed to concentrate on pursuing his career instead of pursuing his fellow female co-workers.

Another evaluation was given to a student without anything written on the paper. The student inquired why the evaluation wasn't completed. The manager explained that the evaluation would have been completed if the student had completed some work during the program.

A female manager completed a male student's evaluation, and at the end of her written comments, she left her phone number and a note asking to hook up before he went home. The student followed through with his manager's request.

A Fall, 1996 alumna recalls: "My evaluation said I needed to improve on my attitude, learn responsibility, show up for work at my next job and decrease the number of times I call-in sick. At the very bottom of the written comments my manager wrote, 'Come back anytime!' I guess I wasn't that bad."

A Spring, 1998 alumnus remembers: "I was probably the worst CP in our area, but my manager gave me a perfect evaluation. When he handed it to me, I asked if he made a mistake. He informed me that I always kept him on his toes and never made his day a boring experience. After all, I was the guy who vomited on his white shirt."

A Fall, 2003 alumnus recalls: "My manager wrote, 'Please don't ever come back.' I asked my manager if there was a problem. He looked at the form and was taken aback. He accidentally wrote that on my evaluation while he was speaking with a guest over the telephone."

~

Costumes must be returned to the company, and other last minute loose ends must be tied up before students are released back into the real world. Some students believe they are allowed to keep company property. One student stole a Haunted Mansion costume with full intentions of wearing it for future Halloween parties.

Another student attempted to steal five different costumes from the Magic Kingdom. Security confronted the young girl, and she explained that Disney told her it would be okay to borrow her new wardrobe.

One student asked her manager if she could borrow her Pirates' costume for a year. When asked why she wanted to borrow the costume, the student explained it was to be a fun surprise for her boyfriend back home. The request wasn't granted.

In a separate act of theft, a student asked his manager if he could take home his Space Mountain costume as a souvenir. The manager declined the request but the student attempted to steal the costume anyway. Approaching his car in the parking lot, the student pulled out the costume and began placing it in his car's backseat. The student's manager had followed him and caught the unethical act in progress.

Costumes may be the number one item stolen from the Walt Disney World Resort, but students also attempt to smuggle out other souvenirs on their last day as well. One curious student believed he could take home the Main Street U.S.A. Emporium cash register. The student attempted to break off the cash register from the counter. After the student's attempted robbery, he explained that he wanted to see how difficult it would be for cast members to steal a cash register. Local authorities were called-in, and the student was taken away for his actions. He failed to return to the resort for any future programs.

Another student believed he could take a company vehicle out for a joyride on his last night of work. After security quickly caught the thief, the student explained that he was testing the vehicle for future College Program students.

In yet another odd incident, an unusual student was caught stealing dust from the Haunted Mansion. Security was unaware of how to go about completing a report on the stolen dust, so they released the student.

Two honest students decided to steal company stationery. After realizing how low and unethical it was to steal paper, the two students returned the company stationery but got caught in the process of making the return. Both students were terminated from the program.

A Fall, 2004 alumnus recalls: "My roommate stole his Star Tours costume and I asked him why he'd ever want to wear a Disney costume outside of Walt Disney World. He explained that the costume would give him prestige among his friends back home."

A Fall, 2005 alumnus asks: "How can students make it to their last day of work and risk everything by stealing something that is worthless? One of my roommates got caught stealing his costume and he was terminated on his second to last day."

~

There are students who check-out early from the program before their official departure date arrives. Terminations and mysterious disappearances within months, weeks or even days before the end of a student's program are baffling. One hard-working student survived the program until his last two days when he suddenly decided the program wasn't for him. He quit with one day of work and two days of living at Vista Way remaining.

During one fall semester a student mysteriously quit with four days remaining in the program. No one knew exactly what had happened, but the rumor circulating suggested it was because he poisoned Disney CEO Michael Eisner's cookies. There is no confirmation whether poisoned cookies were involved.

Another student quit the program with two days remaining because her boyfriend, a fellow student, dumped her. She couldn't deal with the bad situation for two more days.

In a rather odd incident, a student mysteriously disappeared as he didn't show up to his scheduled shift. Rumors began circulating that the student received a Level Five Termination. From that point on, he was known as the CP who got a "Level Five," and no one really knew for what Level Five Termination stood.

Then there's the student who decided he had enough of the program with only two weeks remaining. He told his managers that Disney lied to him about the place being magical. He provided no other reason and left the program.

A Fall, 2002 alumna recalls: "I quit the program with two weeks remaining because I couldn't tolerate Disney any longer. After I left, I realized how big of a mistake I made because I missed it. I went back the following year to do a second program."

A Spring, 2003 alumnus remembers: "I quit the program with one week remaining because I wanted to see my girlfriend. I returned home, saw her and realized that I loved the program much more. I dumped my girlfriend and returned to Florida permanently."

A Fall, 2004 alumna recalls: "Our roommate quit her job but stayed in the apartment for three weeks. Housing officials finally kicked her out."

~

Moving out of the apartments is an event in itself. The atmosphere is quite a sight as Vista Way, Chatham Square, The Commons, and Patterson Court empty out. Some students remain as they either extend their program or remain a few extra days, depending upon their official check-out date.

Students are required to clean their living quarters from top to bottom and inspect every piece of furnishing for lost or damaged items. Four students quickly cleaned their apartment by placing all of their excess belongings left behind under their beds. Unknown to the students was that amidst the junk was $100 which was found by housing officials one day after the students returned home.

After cleaning their apartment spotlessly, six roommates decided they needed to have one last party before they left. A spotless apartment turned into a complete mess within one hour. The students didn't clean the apartment the second time around and were charged for their little going away party.

In a rather startling discovery, a student was pulling off his bed sheets and discovered a used condom underneath the sheet. He later learned that the used condom belonged to his roommate and had been there for a few weeks.

After scrubbing their bathroom from top to bottom the night before their check-out date, two students left for dinner and returned one hour later. Their roommate had vomited all over the clean bathroom floor. Unfortunately, the students had to clean the bathroom all over again.

Suitcases become packed with more items than students bring with them, automobiles are jammed with personal belongings, and last minute good-byes are made. One student packed his suitcase so tightly that while walking down from the third floor, the suitcase exploded under pressure and sent his clothes flying all over the ground. Immediately, a thunderstorm hit the area.

Another student decided that throwing his large suitcase down to his car from the third floor was more convenient. After launching the suitcase, another student walked past the intended target and got pegged in the face by the large piece of luggage. The injured student received only a bloody nose.

CHECKING-OUT

As two students carried their television down the stairs, they finished the last flight of stairs, suddenly tripped and went skidding down the rest of the way. Both students survived but the television didn't make the trip.

One spring afternoon, a student was in such a hurry to leave the complex that she quickly drove her vehicle off property. During her quick exit, she turned a corner and slammed into two vacuum cleaners and a pile of luggage. Without stopping, she continued driving away from the scene while her vehicle dragged one of the vacuum cleaners from its rear until a security host at the main gate could stop her.

In a separate incident, one student drove away in her tightly packed van, but the back door sprang open and left a trail of clothing all the way back to the property exit. Nearby students flagged her down, and the group helped clean up the mess.

A Fall, 2000 alumnus recalls: "The last day was tough. Everyone was in tears and sad to leave. We were all excited about the program coming to an end weeks before, but when it came time to leave we didn't want it to end."

A Spring, 2001 alumna remembers: "I cried most of my last day!"

A fall 2001 alumna recalls: "I drove away, but had to turn back around to say good-bye one more time to my roommates I grew to love."

A Spring, 2005 alumna states: "Checking-out is a process, not an event. Everyone arrives on different dates, so they leave on different dates as well. Saying good-bye is really a two-week process. It's sad, emotional, and terrifying because most students don't know what may happen to them after their program concludes."

~

There are times in the program which students believe are the worst parts. As the last day concludes and students return home, they realize the worst part of their program experience has just occurred. For most, stepping foot on an airplane or in one's own home symbolizes the end of a great experience. Many students experience culture shock, while some need a few days to re-adjust to the real world. After all, students have been *Mouse-Washed* and institutionalized for an extensive period of time.

Students hang pictures on their walls and scrapbook their picture albums. Family and friends inquire about all of the adventures and memories experienced in the program. Students enjoy revealing their adventures, but family and friends just don't understand the real experience and the impact the program has had upon them.

A Fall, 2003 alumnus recalls: "I'd tell my friends all of the stories, but they just didn't understand because they weren't there like I was."

A Fall, 2005 alumna states: "I'd share my stories, but they just didn't 'click' with anyone. I'd have to call my roommates from the program to relive all of the memories, good and bad."

~

Students become so *Mouse-Washed* from the program that they bring the Disney mindset home with them. After months of Disney routines and continuous *Disney Speak*, it takes a few weeks and sometimes months before the pixie dust fades away.

CHECKING-OUT

A Fall, 1996 alumna states: "Re-adjusting to home is the toughest part!"

A Fall, 1999 alumna recalls: "It was tough for about a month to re-adjust. I expected to drink and party at Pleasure Island every Thursday night. I woke up one morning thinking that I was going to the beach with my friends."

Another Fall, 2000 alumna remembers: "I'd always point with two fingers, the Disney point. One day on campus I pointed directions for a guy and he thought I gave him a nonverbal sexual message."

A Fall, 2001 alumnus recalls: "I used the Disney point while giving directions to a lady. She noticed how I was pointing and asked if I worked for Disney."

A Spring, 2002 alumnus remembers: "I used Disney Speak in my everyday language and it would catch people's attention. I referred to a customer at work as a guest. She appreciated it."

A Fall, 2003 alumnus recalls: "I'd come out of my bedroom and expect to see my roommates from the program. It took about two weeks to readjust."

A Fall, 2004 alumnus remembers: "I walked out to the kitchen and saw a mess of dishes my parents had left. I remember telling my parents that my roommates from the program were cleaner than they were."

A Spring, 2005 alumnus states: "No matter where they're from, every student goes home saying 'ya'll.' I lived in Oregon and I said 'ya'll' for another five months after I returned home."

~

Students successfully completing the Disney College Program have the opportunity to return to it. For those having withdrawals from Disney and the Florida sunshine, several options are made available to program alumni for their return to the magical kingdom. Disney's flexibility might be attributed to its continuing need for cheap labor, and students jump at the opportunities. Depending on students' work status, they may request to extend their program stay. For the students who aren't ready to return to the real world or just can't get enough of Mickey and Minnie Mouse, extending is the logical choice.

If students choose to extend, they should do so for the right reasons. After getting into an argument with her parents over the telephone a few weeks before her program concluded, a student extended so she wouldn't have to live with her parents. She never returned home and made Florida her permanent residence. One year later, however, her parents retired and moved to the Orlando area.

Another student extended because she was dating a young man who worked at Epcot. One day after she extended, the fellow broke off their relationship.

In a more common reason, one poor student extended because she didn't have enough money to drive back home to Nevada. She learned her lesson and saved enough money during her second program so she could get back home.

A Fall, 2003 alumnus recalls: "I 'extended' my program because I didn't want to go back home where there was two-feet of snow waiting."

A Spring, 2004 alumna remembers: "I couldn't return home because I left everything and started a new life in Florida. I 'extended' my program and after four months I was promoted to a Guest Service Manager role."

~

Students may apply to become a Campus Representative of the Disney College Program at their college or university. Campus Representatives are official *MarketEARs* of the program and help Disney recruiters promote the program for future students. The position offers no compensation, but Campus Representatives keep their benefits such as free theme park admission and discounts. The position also makes for a great resume builder.

A Fall, 2002 Campus Representative remembers: "I got the best of both worlds by living at home, but still working for Disney. I learned a lot about marketing and promoting."

A Fall, 2003 Campus Representative recalls: "I'd place flyers on all of the local pizza parlors' boxes. Everyone in my town knew about the Disney College Program when I was a Campus Representative."

A Spring, 2004 Campus Representative states: "Being a Campus Rep. is a cheap way for Disney to promote the program but it works very well!"

~

What used to be referred to as Advanced Internships are now called Professional Internships. These high caliber positions are available to applicants, and selected positions are only available to College Program alumni. These internships cater more toward students choosing a career path with The Walt Disney Company.

The Professional Internships offer a slightly higher level of compensation than most students' first positions with Disney. Past students have obtained management, engineering, and entertainment internships with the company.

College Program alumni can choose to return to the resort for summer positions as well. Students may work a three month season if they have a favorable re-hire status. A small selection of roles are available.

A Fall, 2003 Management Professional Intern recalls: "I worked hard in my Disney College Program, networked with everyone, faced diversity, got an Advanced Internship and now I'm an Area Manager in Operations."

A Summer, 2009 alumnus remembers: "I went back to work during the summer. It provides you with that quick Disney fix and works well with one's school schedule."

~

The Disney College Program could very well be Walt Disney's original concept of Epcot, The Experimental Prototype Community of Tomorrow. Students from all around the world live and work in a community where students rent their living space. Everyone in the community must work in order to live. Learning experiences are provided daily, and transportation is available to those needing the service. It's by no means a perfect match to Walt's original concept but very similar in what he envisioned. The Disney College Program is essentially the real Epcot, The Experimental Prototype "College" of Today.

Today, the Disney College Program continues to attract thousands of young students each year for a magical once-in-a-lifetime experience. The program is highly valuable to both Disney and students. Disney continues to fill the resort with cheap labor, to teach young students the values of a Fortune 100 Company, and to train future leaders of the company. Students leave the program with lasting memories, new friendships, and lessons in the practical aspects of life.

The next time you visit the Walt Disney World Resort, ask a few young cast members if they've received their *Ducktorate*. Ask them how much they enjoy living at Vista Way. Or, ask them how much they're enjoying their time in sunny Florida. No matter how honest or dishonest their responses may be, you will see a smile on their faces that can't lie, a smile that indicates deep down they're having the time of their lives.

Walt Disney once stated: "You can dream, create, design and build the most wonderful place in the world...but it requires people to make that dream a reality."

A large number of these people are indeed Disney College Program students.

Chapter Nine

The Journey

The way to get started is to quit talking and begin doing.
—Walt Disney

Every student has a different experience in his or her college program. Some of those experiences are good, others are bad, and yet others may be somewhere in between. Many students partake in all the craziness that the program may offer while others choose to stay away from the extreme craziness. The program has an impact on every student, and many students have similar experiences, feelings, and expectations throughout the duration of their program. The following three memoirs share what the program is all about, from start to finish, through a narrative approach. The first memoir is from a 2005-2006 alumna. The second memoir is from a Fall, 2008 alumnus. The third memoir is from the author's Fall, 2003 experience.

~

2005-2006 Alumna Memoir

Ever since I could remember, I've had an interest in Disney. According to my parents I started liking Disney as soon as I had an understanding of the world. As a very young child, all the children on the block and classmates played with Barbies and other child-related products. I was right at home with Mickey Mouse, Donald Duck, and Goofy. These were the icons of my adolescence.

I graduated high school, and like so many other young adults, had no clue what I wanted to study during my first year of college let alone what I wanted for a career. During my sophomore year of college, it was brought to my attention by a flyer at my college campus that the Disney College Program would be holding a presentation at the local state college, some five miles away. Naturally, I was interested.

Late one afternoon in March, 2005, I attended a presentation that would change my life. I attended the event with many others, and just like I had expected, I was completely sold on the program. I went home to dinner that night completely boasting and raving about the program. To my parents' credit, they listened intently as I shared my dream.

Now that I was set on attending the program, I had to initiate phase two of the process. I needed to interview and be accepted into the program. Interviews were two weeks after I first heard about the program, so I had little time to practice my public speaking skills and brush up on every piece of knowledge regarding the program and Disney in general.

The night before my interview, I couldn't fall asleep. I felt as if the weight of the world was resting on my shoulders. This had been my dream, to always be a part of Disney in some small way, shape, or form, and I finally had the chance. I prayed that I didn't stumble over my words or get tricked up by some questions that might have popped up. Low and behold I was accepted into the program. I left for Walt Disney World in August, 2005 and arrived two days before I was to begin. Little did I know that not only was I in for the time of my life, but also I would soon gain both experiences and friendships that would last a lifetime.

~

I was assigned to work at Soarin'. It was an exciting time for me as the ride was brand new to Epcot, and I was literally working in the theme park that I had wanted to work in.

For those of you who may not be aware, Soarin' is an attraction which simulates hang gliding. Suspended fifty-feet in the air, a giant IMAX screen is directly in front of the guest and displays images of California. The experience takes guests over the Golden Gate Bridge in San Francisco, Redwood Creek in Humboldt County, the wine country in Napa, the coastline of Monterey, Lake Tahoe, Yosemite National Park, the PGA West golf course in La Quinta, Camarillo, Anza-Borrego Desert State Park, San Diego, Malibu, Los Angeles, and lastly Disneyland at holiday time. What makes the ride special, in my view, are the smells that are pumped forth as the guests journey on their California hang-gliding adventure. The smell of oranges, the sea, pine trees, and the river is present as guests work their way over many landmarks.

The first day at work was extremely difficult. It was a blast, but being on your feet for countless hours was a challenge. The secret lay in the fact that I needed to learn how to stand with bent knees, a tactic that I began using each day. This lessened the strain on my knees. Nonetheless, I found the strength to get through the first day and eventually the first week.

That first night I was practically asleep before my head even hit the pillow. I had the time of my life, but my body ached from the constant standing and fatigue, and I lost my voice due to the constant talking I needed to do over the large crowds of people. My body ached and my voice was sore, but I closed my eyes that night knowing that I was in the exact place on Earth where I wanted to be.

My first week in the program went by in a flash. I worked hard each day. Guests were demanding and my managers expected quite a bit from me. I liked knowing that I could make it in an environment that was fast-paced. I noticed that my own expectations of myself had also increased dramatically as well. I had gone into the program thinking that it was just another job, but I was being trained in a multitude of different fields. My public speaking skills were improving day-by-day along with my confidence. I felt more comfortable in front of large groups of people. I was beginning to "soar" and found out just how competent I was. I felt confident, and it showed in how I was carrying myself. My customer service skills were improving as well, and my problem solving skills began to sharpen each day.

During my first week, I began knowing my co-workers both on as well off the job. At first it was a little relentless. It seemed as if all I did was work long day after long day, and the only time I had for getting to know my co-workers on a more personal level was in the breakroom during those first few days. I'd often socialize with whoever it was that was also on break with me. Casual conversations would usually break into laughter as I got to know my fellow co-workers better and better, and many of those breakroom talks usually led to hanging out on weekends and free time. These conversations became the basis of many of my relationships and friendships that I developed there.

The friends that I was acquiring came from a multitude of backgrounds and ethnicities. Some were current college students like I, and others had been out in the work world for quite some time. What I enjoyed most was that I was meeting people from all over the United States as well as from all over the world. Many of my closer friends came from Ohio, Texas, and Illinois, to name just a few. They attended universities such as Ohio State, University of Illinois, and the University of Texas. As someone who had spent my entire lifetime living in California, I found it thoroughly refreshing to be meeting people who were from different backgrounds. Many of my friends had accents, and it was fun to know that not only was I acquiring a new network of friends, but I was also gaining and learning deep insights into different cultures.

~

Customer service was exceedingly important while performing my job. There were new demands each and every day while at work. Often people would approach me and try to bribe me with cash to let them cut ahead in line. While I can't say that this always was done with integrity and the best interests at mind, I can say that I never accepted a bribe, and I'm very proud of this. Many were not as strong-willed as I was.

People would ask for all sorts of strange requests, from dancing and entertaining them while they waited in line, to listening to their failed businesses or failed marriages. Most of the time, people merely wanted a person to whom they could vent their feelings and frustrations, and, unfortunately many of my co-workers and I were those people. I mean, let me tell you, I heard it all. From love affairs to the use of Viagra, I believe I heard everything and anything under the sun.

While many people who did come through the gates at Soarin' were in a fantastic mood, others were not. While we always engaged with everyone and did our best to deliver an outstanding experience, it was the individuals and families who were in a bad mood that we tried to win over and change their day around.

The disgruntled guests and unhappy people with whom I dealt were those whose experience our managers hoped we could change. It was important for us to ensure that each guest became a repeat customer through positive experiences. It was up to all of us cast members to turn these guests' terrible days into magical ones. A guest who exits the park disgruntled may not return, and this is bad for the Disney brand in many ways. Maybe that individual or individuals will never buy another piece of Disney merchandise or go to see a Disney movie again. My managers wanted me to start seeing the guest experience in this light. Once they clued me in to this way of thinking, I realized how important every interaction and discussion was.

~

The months went by quickly for me as I got into a rhythm of going to work and putting in a good effort. Parties soon became the norm as everyone was either attending one or throwing one. I had never been much of a big partier, and during college I never was, so I look at my time spent in the program as getting all the partying out of my system.

Drinking was heavily present in the program and some individuals took in far too much of it. For many of my friends and me, the Ale House became a popular place. We also took great advantage of the World Showcase and would often spend many nights going from country to country sampling food and beverages.

After two months in the program, I began to miss home. It was the first true time that I had been away from home. It's often said that in life it's not the job that keeps someone around but the actual friendships and relationships that are built. I can say that in my case this was true. There were times when the job had me down, my managers demanded quite a bit, and the unrelenting guests were absolutely brutal. What got me through these hard times were the friends that I had made, and the friendships that I was cultivating.

Many of my friends held jobs that weren't only mundane and repetitive but downright disgusting. I had a number of friends whose job it was to bus and clean the tables at all the eating establishments throughout the park. People can be absolutely filthy when it comes to food and leaving their garbage around. Picture a family of six, with two adults and four young children eating a meal consisting of hamburgers, drinks, and fries. Now picture tons of opened ketchup and mustard packets all over the place. Many of these tables were so dirty that you wouldn't want to walk on them, let alone eat on top of them. For most of my friends the only things that kept them sane and remaining in the program were the close bonds and relationships formed during the experience.

~

I approached the last two weeks of my time in the program with a bit of uncertainty. I was happy to be going home, but I knew I would be leaving all the friends I made as well as my love and affection for the park and the Disney brand itself. My parents and brother visited me once during my fall program and I thoroughly enjoyed the visit. They were able to see me in my element, to see how confident I had become, and, to see how I had grown in maturity. I was grateful that I had them witness me "in action" as many of my co-workers never had those personal visits from home.

During my final two weeks, I did my best to soak it all in. I wanted to take in every last sight, smell, sound, and experience. I knew once I returned home, it would be all over and I'd go back to living my normal lifestyle. I'm not saying that my life at home was boring, but let's face it; it's not like living in a theme park. When you spend four months out of your life living in Walt Disney World, it really does feel like living in Fantasyland. This isn't to say that once you enter the confines of any of the parks, all your worries and problems go away. However, it's the only place that I can think of where for that day life is magical for the millions who go through the turnstiles each year. There is something magical about all the theme parks, and any Disney fan or enthusiast would attest to this.

During my last week many of my co-workers and friends knew that I'd be leaving, and they proceeded to throw me a going away party each night of the week for the entire week. While it also may just have been another opportunity for them to go out and have a good time, I wasn't one to pass up a good time either. For seven nights straight my friends and co-workers went out each night and celebrated my program's conclusion. By this time I had already added everyone I knew from the parks onto my Facebook page. As I'd soon find out over the subsequent years, this would be my source of communication with many of these individuals.

My last day finally arrived, and I was more than sad. I was downright scared to leave Disney. The one thing that cheered me up was that I made up my mind that I'd return to take part in the program again. I finished my four month assignment in January 2006, and by May, 2006, I had returned once again for another experience in the Alumni Summer Program. After graduation from college, I returned again in January 2008 to do the Spring program prior to my entrance into graduate school in fall of that year.

Counting my three internship programs and countless personal visits to the park, I've now spent over one and a half years of my life living in the Disney confines. And one year in this magical place is simply not enough.

Fall, 2008 Alumnus Memoir

I never imagined living and working in a theme park. I was studying political science and was a pre-law student at a prominent university on the east coast. I was living in the dorms and having the time of my life in the college world. It was a perfect world in my eyes, and nothing could change this. What was I thinking?

I agreed to attend a campus presentation with a friend who was interested in the Disney College Program. After attending the presentation I was hooked and decided to sign up for an interview. My interview occurred one day later and after answering some pretty easy questions I knew I'd get accepted. My friend and I got my acceptance letter about one month after the interview. My friend immediately accepted the internship. I logged in on the program's official Web site and was about to decline the offer. I almost clicked the button and then it hit me; what the hell, why not?

~

August, 2008 arrived, and I was off to Florida. My friend had to cancel his program acceptance at the last minute due to a family emergency. This would be a first for me because this was my first trip to Florida and my first visit to a Disney theme park. When I crossed the Florida state line, I almost turned my car around to go back home but I kept driving.

After signing in and getting my official room assignment, I knew that this was for real. I was assigned to work at the Magic Kingdom's Pirates of the Caribbean. I heard of the attraction, but never knew any details about it. I was so nervous on my first day

I parked next to a fire hydrant by mistake. Apartment security informed me of my mistake and I began unpacking my car.

I got settled into my two bedroom apartment at Vista Way. I met my roommates and we instantly hit it off. Once they learned that I'd never visited a Disney theme park, they dragged me to the Magic Kingdom that night. It was here that I saw what I was in for. We walked past Pirates of the Caribbean and I freaked out. They couldn't possibly expect me to wear that terrible looking pirate costume.

After going through *Traditions* and other trainings, I was provided with my work schedule. My first day and week had its challenges, and I eventually got used to wearing a pirate costume. I don't think I slept for a week because of the work schedule, parties, and theme park visits.

Looking back, my favorite part of the experience was the friendships and large network of contacts I made at work and out-of-work. I had my fair share of crazy moments in the program. I was so drunk one night I accidently locked myself out of my apartment. Without thinking I just decided to sleep on the door mat until morning. Everyone else inside was passed out. My craziest moment at work was when a guest accused me of stealing her purse. I explained to the guest that I didn't do such a thing, but she was positive that I took it. She got her husband, and he came over to threaten me. He said I had one chance at returning it or he'd kick my ass. Luckily there were two security hosts nearby who intervened. It turned out that the guest left her purse in the bathroom across the way.

As the months went on, I got to experience the holidays and the large crowds who visited the resort. The only way to unwind from the madness would be the friendships. The friendships led to social functions, and the social functions led to extracurricular activity. I met my wife while I was in the program. We began dating during my last month and got married in Spring, 2009. She worked on the Jungle Cruise. While I lived at Vista Way, she lived at Chatham Square. There were times when it was difficult to meet because of the 1:00 A.M. rule, but we always found sneaky ways to get around this rule.

~

My time in the program quickly concluded, and it felt like I just started. I knew that I wouldn't come back for a career with Disney because I was focused on law school. I knew that I wouldn't extend or participate in a second program as well. During my final days, I made the best of my time and took every opportunity the program presented. My friends were in tears, and I had a tear as well. It was definitely one of the toughest times I had experienced in life. The program leaves an impact on you in ways one can't imagine until they experience the magic.

When I think back to my program experience, I know that there were both good and bad times, but the good outnumbered the bad. The worst part of the experience was the pay. The best part quickly made one forget about the pay and that was the numerous friendships made during the program. Many of these friendships are still alive and well within my life today. The most important friend I made was indeed my wife. And to think, I almost turned the car around after crossing the state line.

Author's Memoir

It was a warm April afternoon as I sat in Los Angeles traffic that was moving no faster than thirty miles per hour. My classes had concluded for the day at UCLA, and I was desperately trying to get home. My cell phone rang, and I answered. It was a friend of mine who worked at the Disneyland Resort in Anaheim, California. He informed me that all campus presentations for the Walt Disney World College Program had already taken place in and around the Los Angeles area. The closest university was in Northern California about eight hours away, and the presentation was scheduled for the following morning. I drove home, packed a bag, and began the long drive to Northern California later that evening.

That morning, I arrived at the campus with ten minutes to spare and quickly found the room. I walked in and immediately observed three young campus representatives wearing black mouse ears. I took a seat among a group of about fifty eager students. The recruiter stood at the front and introduced what the *Living*, *Learning* and *Earning* components of the program were all about. The anxious group, including me, was intrigued at the possibilities of living on Walt Disney World Resort property while working in an internship that was unique in several ways. A short video was presented, and it was the typical scripted brainwashing material but everyone was still very interested. The time came to schedule an interview, and the large group began pushing its way through to seize the opportunity. After the group thinned out, I scheduled my interview for the following morning and would have the evening to make final preparations.

The morning of the big interview arrived, and I sat in a lobby waiting for the recruiter to call my name. A young and very professional woman called me back, and I quickly jumped to my feet. I sat on one side of a table while she sat on the other side. The enthusiastic recruiter informed me that I'd be the only candidate. I was really looking forward to a group interview but had no complaints. We discussed the opportunities in the program and my work experience with the Disneyland Resort. We discussed several projects I worked on with team members and how my time spent at UCLA was beneficial. She asked what roles I'd prefer and what living arrangements I was interested in. I explained that I wanted to work as a Park Greeter at the Magic

Kingdom and wanted a two-bedroom wellness apartment located at Vista Way. She was taken aback at how knowledgeable I was about the program and the role I wanted. She claimed that she would try her best in meeting my requests. After a thirty minute conversation, the interview concluded, and I was on the road back to the Los Angeles area.

The end of April approached, and I had yet to hear a decision. Concerned thoughts about my chances of being accepted into the program crossed my mind. The first week of May arrived, and I was offered an internship on my birthday. The acceptance letter informed me that I would be cast into an Operations role, but I knew that it could be as a Park Greeter, in Attractions or in a Parking role. I was still unaware of which theme park I'd be assigned to or whether my living requests would be granted. I accepted the offer and chose an arrival date of August 20, 2003. I had over two months to prepare for the four-month adventure.

~

As I sat in the airport waiting to board my flight to Orlando, Florida, I knew it wasn't too late to turn around and go back home. Nerves and doubts of traveling to an unknown location began spreading through my mind, and then it was time to board my flight. I grabbed my carry-on luggage, placed my nerves aside, and just did it; I got on the airplane and never looked back.

I arrived at Orlando International Airport (MCO) around 4:00 P.M. and looked out of the airplane window, only to discover it was raining quite heavily. I walked off the airplane, and it instantly hit me; it was hotter than hell. My perspiration increased as the sticky air caused by the ninety percent humidity was immediately in effect. I couldn't understand how it was pouring rain with a temperature of ninety degrees. I quickly adapted to the unfamiliar climate before I even stepped outside of the airport.

After waiting forty-five minutes for my over-packed suitcase to arrive on the luggage belt, I boarded a shuttle bus and was on my way to the Walt Disney World Resort. I acted as if I had been to Florida several times before, when, in reality, it was only the second visit in my very young life. I arrived at a hotel which was about a half-mile from Vista Way. My check-in date wouldn't be until the following morning.

~

The alarm went off but I was already wide-awake from a sleepless night. I walked out onto the room's balcony and stood there for a few moments as I gathered my thoughts about the day ahead. I was still amazed at this odd but wonderful climate. It was 6:00 A.M. and the temperature was no cooler than eighty-five degrees with a humidity of ninety percent. I got ready for the long day and quickly walked down to the hotel lobby. I was too excited and a little nervous to eat breakfast. Without thinking of getting a shuttle or taxi, I began walking to Vista Way. I dragged my two pieces of luggage along the side of the road as I attempted to conquer the half-mile trip. Any other time, a half-mile would have been like a walk in the park. This particular walk, however, was more difficult than I could have imagined. My shirt was drenched in sweat, caused by the humidity, and the wheels on my heavy suitcase wouldn't properly work.

I finally arrived at the Vista Way entrance and was directed to the check-in location. All I could think about was when I could possibly get rid of my heavy suitcase. A friendly cast member welcomed me and was my new best friend because she informed me of an area where I could place my luggage. I was also getting hungry and regretted skipping breakfast. After checking-in, I received some paperwork and my room assignment. I learned that my recruiter followed through and met my requests. I was cast into a Park Greeter role at the Magic Kingdom and assigned to a two-bedroom wellness apartment. Perhaps I should have asked for a higher pay rate, too.

Before I located my apartment, I obtained my housing identification card and met some new people. It was here that I'd meet my best friend while in the program and what would eventually turn out to be one of my best friends, period. Jim, an older student who just broke thirty, was a child at heart. A few years before the program, he served our country in the military and was nearly killed in the line-of-duty. After getting out of the service, he wouldn't use the excuse of "it's too late for college" and began working on his college degree. We weren't assigned to the same apartment, but perhaps that was a good thing because who knows if we would have become such good friends if we lived together.

I began searching for my apartment building in the oddly designed complex. The building numbers weren't in order, and it was like navigating through a difficult maze. I finally found my third floor apartment, carried my luggage up the stairs, and entered as the door was wide open. Two other guys were in the process of carrying personal items into their bedroom, and the guy sharing the room with me was unpacking his suitcase.

My immediate roommate reminded me of a young Anthony Soprano from HBO's *The Sopranos*. Anthony, in his twenties, an Italian culinary student, was the chef in the apartment. We called him Butta, and it was the perfect nickname. He wore his hats without creasing the brims and always wore long, baggy shirts. His New York upbringing and Bronx demeanor were visibly present. His well-mannered and polite personality combined with his high level of intelligence was a welcomed sight. The kid was a pure genius.

My other two roommates were Derek, or Deke, as we called him, and Zach. Both were from New York. Deke was the talented actor in the group, and Zach was going to be the next great Disney *Imagineer*. Anthony and I walked into their bedroom to talk with the two of them and immediately noticed something different about the room; the two beds were pushed together. Our immediate reaction consisted of shock and curiosity, but we both quickly came to the realization that our two roommates were homosexual.

Before I began the program I never had any prejudices toward the homosexual community. My belief was that everyone is a human being and some just choose a different lifestyle. Sure, that's what everybody says but does anyone really mean it? Was I really okay with having two homosexual roommates? After a few days of settling into the apartment, Deke and Zach instantly became two great roommates and two great people. They were two of the nicest and most intriguing individuals I met while in the program. I learned a great deal from them, and I couldn't have asked for two better individuals to know.

Here I was, sharing a room with three guys from New York. I was the outsider, the surfer boy all the way from California. The apartment was very diverse in other areas as well. Butta and I were the clean ones while Deke and Zach were just learning how to clean up after they made a mess. It wasn't the fault of Zac and Deke. Butta and I were just border-line OCD. There were times when Butta and I needed to remind the two that the trash needed to be taken out when overflowing, and the kitchen didn't clean up by itself. Butta was the one who snored, and I was the one who had routine nightmares. I remember during one of my first few nights, I had a horrific nightmare and woke up screaming, "Bats, bats! There are bats in the room!" Butta woke up and yelled, "Shut the fuck up!" I fell back to sleep and didn't have another nightmare for years.

~

I remember my days in the program quite vividly. Jim and I would go grocery shopping at 2:00 A.M. and it was always at Wal-Mart, or as Butta called it, "Wal-Marts." Nothing was greater than driving down SR535 at 2:00 A.M., with all of the windows rolled down, allowing the warm air to hit our faces and having *Van Halen* blasting out of the speakers.

I was introduced to Steak n' Shake and immediately fell in love with the food. I was notorious for ordering a steak burger, cup of chili, fries, a strawberry milkshake, and a coke. Yes, it was all of that food in one sitting. Steak n' Shake came in handy after late night visits to Pleasure Island, Downtown Disney, midnight movies at the Downtown Disney AMC, the theme parks, or a long day at work. Butta suggested I buy stock in Steak n' Shake as he swore the stock price increased on the days I'd eat there.

I learned a great deal about cultures and how to live with people. Learning to understand, to appreciate, and to respect others' beliefs and values was a lesson that couldn't be taught in a university classroom. Butta taught me to stick up for myself and to be tough with every situation I faced. Deke taught me the power of laughter and how making others laugh is a great gift to possess. Lastly, Jim showed me how New York drivers navigate the roads while behind the wheel of an automobile. Tourists would quickly get out of Jim's way when he was behind the wheel.

~

As I walked down Main Street U.S.A. with one of my managers in late November, the building lights began shutting off. It was 2:00 A.M., the park was cleared out, and we were the last two people remaining on Main Street U.S.A. The dark castle stood quietly in the distance as the full moon illuminated the street giving us just enough light to navigate the deserted area. My manager turned to me and explained how lucky he was to be able to close Main Street U.S.A. in the Magic Kingdom. I remember thinking that not too many people have such an opportunity and I was one of the selected few allowed to experience that Disney magic.

During my four months of the *Earning* experience, I learned more than I ever had before. I was spit on by guests, my toe was run over and broken by an electronic wheel chair, and I worked quite a few fifteen hour shifts. A few peers and I figured out how to manipulate the Cast Deployment System (CDS) so that we were given several fifteen minute breaks during our shifts. I had my share of call-ins for the various beach trips and parties. I even sneaked into the Magic Kingdom on a day I called-in sick. I met many wonderful students who all had great futures in whatever they chose to do. I networked with every cast member I could have imagined; the Vice-President of Walt Disney World Resort Operations, the Vice-President and General Manager of the Magic Kingdom, several entry-level executives, and many more.

I reported to five Guest Service Managers, but there was one manager who was always there for me and became my mentor. Craig, one of Disney's finest, was a soft-spoken leader who treated every cast member like a true human being. Every student and cast member trusted him and looked up to him as a true leader. His knowledge and personality quickly inspired me, and, to this day, I still apply much of the knowledge which he shared with me. Craig is a leader that the Walt Disney World Resort could never afford to lose.

As Jim and I stood at the edge of the World Showcase lagoon in Epcot, Illuminations: Reflections of Earth was moments away from beginning, and my college program was hours away from concluding. I began reflecting on my last four months of an incredible journey that changed my life. I remembered the warm fall nights during the *Mickey's Not So Scary Halloween Parties*, the cool evenings during the Thanksgiving holiday week, and the time I took on a bet where I drank one gallon of turkey gravy at our Main Street U.S.A. Daily Operations Thanksgiving dinner. The friendships I made and the experiences that I'd remember for a lifetime all went through my mind. I was proud to earn my *Ducktorate* degree and honored to learn all I did through my networking experiences. Illuminations began as the lights slowly dimmed around the World Showcase lagoon and so, too, on my program.

~

I sat on the long airplane ride home wanting the plane to immediately turn around. I was scared of no longer living behind the walls of Vista Way or walking down Main Street U.S.A. after hours in the warm, humid climate. The thought of not being able to see my program friends and colleagues the following day was terrifying. Ironically, I was scared before I arrived in Florida but I was more scared of returning home.

One thing remains present with me today and probably is true among most alumni who have participated in the College Program; I miss the pixie dust and the magical moments that are provided daily at the Walt Disney World Resort. There will always be a place in my heart that holds the memories of my Disney College Program experience, and, there are times when I wonder how I can break back into that special place called Mousecatraz.

Glossary

Adventure
A ride or entertaining experience at a Vista Lay apartment complex.

Alpha-Unit
A Disney code for the ambulance that picks up the student that just passed out after working a fifteen hour shift.

Attraction
A ride or entertaining experience on the way to work or home via a Disney College Program bus.

Backstage
An area not accessible to guests due to Mickey Mouse having a cigarette while talking about last night's party with Pluto.

Cast Deployment System (CDS)
A computerized system designed to issue breaks, job assignments and other work-related tasks. Cast members may request to "Extend" or "Early Release" via the system. The system does all the thinking for the managers.

Cast Member
A Disney employee at a theme park or a resort who works his or her butt off but can never please the guest.

Costume
The themed uniform a cast member is required to wear while working in the ninety degree temperature and one hundred percent humidity.

Disney College Program
An internship program for college students eighteen and older that helps Disney staff its theme parks & resort division without spending too much of its payroll.

Disney Dollars
A form of "fun" currency accepted at Disney theme parks that one student attempted to counterfeit in 2001.

Disney Look
A guideline or list of rules that governs every cast member while at work no matter how hung over they may be from the night before.

Disney Point
A point with the index and middle finger, as opposed to just the index finger. Sometimes cast members would like to use only the middle finger after helping a guest.

Disney University
The Disney cast member training location where students get Mouse-Washed.

GLOSSARY

Ducktorate
A degree awarded to students successfully completing a minimum of one of the Disney College Program Education courses. Not to be mistaken for a Doctorate degree.

Early Released
To be "released" from one's work shift before the scheduled end time so that students can get an early start on a night of partying.

Epcot
The Experimental Prototype College of Today that recruits students from all backgrounds for a Living, Learning, and Earning society all controlled by the Mouse.

Extend
To "extend" one's work shift beyond the scheduled end time so that students can have a few extra dollars after rent is taken out from their small paychecks.

Facade
The face of a building that creates the magical environment at a Disney theme park, or the recruitment presentation that is given to interested applicants on campus and via Internet.

Guest
A customer at the Walt Disney World Resort who not only pays for a cast member's salary but also drives cast members crazy.

Guest Service Manager
A salaried manager who wears nice clothes and pretends to know what he or she is doing.

Imagineer
Term used for the Disney theme parks' engineers who create and build all of the vacation destinations. Formerly known as, "W.E.D. Enterprises."

Learning Laboratory
What the Disney College Program calls the Walt Disney World Resort. The biggest university of which one could think.

MarketEARs
Term used to describe Disney's marketing department when it Mouse Washes guests to buy everything they see.

Merchantainment
Term used to describe the merchandise department that sells the $80 sweatshirts. For a student to save up and purchase, it would take about twelve hours of work.

Mousecatraz
Term used by College Program students to describe the Disney College Program. The term is derived from Alcatraz Island, a former federal prison located in the middle of the San Francisco Bay.

Mousters
A degree awarded to students successfully completing a minimum of forty hours of approved Disney learning activities. Probably worth about the same as a real Master's degree.

Mouse-Washing
A form of Disney brainwashing.

Onstage
Any location where a guest may observe a student creating magical memories or breaking a Disney law.

O-Town
Term used by students in referring to Orlando, Florida.

Protein Spill
Term used to indicate someone has vomited after a crazy party at Vista Way.

Quick-Service
A Disney term for "fast-food" or a Vista Way encounter between two students, sometimes more.

Role
A job or position with Disney that looks good on the resume for other jobs outside of Disney.

Traditions
A form of "Mouse-Washing" that teaches newly hired cast members about The Walt Disney Company's history and philosophies.

Utilidors
The underground tunnels at the Magic Kingdom that cause students to be late for their shift during their first week because of getting lost.

Vista Way
An apartment complex where College Program students are housed. Also known as "Vista Lay."

Notes

--For the privacy of each interviewee the names aren't enclosed. In lieu of names, each student's university has been listed
***Indicates student, cast member, or non-Disney affiliate wished to remain anonymous (including their college affiliation)

Chapter One
Page
4. Speeding candidate, University of California, Los Angeles
5. Counselor, SUNY-Buffalo
Injured student, University of Nevada, Las Vegas
Information booth, University of California, Davis
Lost candidate, University of Miami
6. Confused candidate, Boise State University
Argumentative candidate, Fullerton College
Six Flags employee, Texas State, San Marcos
Terminated employee, California State, Long Beach
7. Smelly candidate, Texas A&M University, Corpus Christi
Cheating student, University of California, Irvine
Dumped candidate, University of Wisconsin, Green Bay
8. Six-foot candidate, University of Washington, Tacoma
Listening candidate, University of Michigan, Ann Arbor
Pet rat, University of Kentucky
9. Bored candidate, California State, Sacramento
Candidate uninterested, University of Maryland, Baltimore
Sex request, California State, San Diego
Mousewashed, University of Connecticut
Interview strategy, California State, Sacramento
10. Great opportunity, University of Georgia, Albany State

11. Inappropriate offer, University of Illinois, Chicago
Wisdom teeth, City of New York, Queens College
A.D.D. candidate, University of Arizona
Walt Disney alive, University of Ohio, Central State
12. R.A. discussion, SUNY-Albany
Crutches interview, California State, San Francisco
Naked tattoo, Washington State, Spokane
Butt tattoo, University of Nevada, Reno
13. No interest, California State, Sacramento
Mickey Mouse religion, California State, San Diego
Jailed candidate, University of Minnesota, Twin Cities
Sexually active candidate, North Dakota State University
Opinionated candidate, University of Arizona
Universal Studios candidate, University of Southern California
14. Nine jobs, Lyon College
Stealing candidate, California State, Los Angeles
Automobile provided, Oklahoma State, Tulsa
Disney pain insurance, California State, Sonoma
Apartment leader, Sterling College
15. Unusual candidate, California State, San Diego
Spoiled candidate, Valley City State University
Termination question, SUNY-Buffalo
Sharing apartment, University of North Alabama
Cell phone candidate, University of California, Los Angeles
16. Magic Mountain candidate, University of California, Los Angeles
Cursing candidate, California State, Long Beach
Rear ended candidate, University of Nebraska, Lincoln
Unethical mouse, Mercer University
17. Misspelled letter, Southeastern University
Disney letter, California State, Chico
Email thank you, University of South Carolina, Union
Wrong address, Penn State, Berks
18. Forgetful candidate, Oregon State University
Unprofessional candidate, California State, San Diego
Confused candidate, University of Wisconsin, Green Bay
Wrong Date, Fullerton College
19. Unlucky student, University of Michigan, Ann Arbor
Mickey Mouse supervisor, California State, San Francisco
"F" grade, Alcorn State University
20. Canadian student, University of Toronto
Borrowed clothing, Montana State, Billings
Forgot underwear, SUNY-Buffalo
Lost luggage, Oklahoma State, Tulsa
Clever student, California State, Bakersfield

Chapter Two
Page

MOUSECATRAZ

Creative student, University of Nebraska, Lincoln
Key West pirates, University of Georgia, Macon State
Special evening, Florida State University
68. Main Street rat, University of Hawaii, Hilo
Mean pirates, University of Tampa
Chucky doll, University of California, Los Angeles & SUNY-Albany
Irish dolls, North Central University
Tower of Terror, University of Nebraska, Omaha
69. Spectromagic, California State, Chico
Park Greeter, SUNY-Fredonia
Dropped tables, Ohio University
Fast-paced show, University of California, Los Angeles
Free tickets, SUNY-Fredonia
70. Special guest, Walsh College
Michael Eisner, LaSalle University
Free parking, ***
Hungry student, University of Mary Washington
71. Cone bowling, SUNY-Albany
Roller blade student, California State, Fullerton
Sleeping student, Austin College
Screaming father, University of Arkansas, Pine Bluff
Upset mother, University of Texas, El Paso
72. Vista Way notes, California State, Chico
Large guest, California State, San Diego
Clumsy student, University of Colorado, Denver
73. Drinking student, Logan University
Food & Beverage student, Rollins College
Free food, ***
Bugs Bunny & Porky Pig, New Mexico State University
74. Stroller baby, University of San Diego
Make a baby, Anderson University
Air-conditioner, California State, San Jose
Disney's Walk Around the World, Peace College
Disney's Leave a Legacy, Wells College
75. Evil fat ass, Western Kentucky University
Human waste, Manchester College
Spaceship Earth Wal-Mart, Coker College
Wally-World Wal-Mart, California State, Chico
76. Disney's Animal Kingdom air-conditioner, SUNY-Buffalo
Random photos, University of Texas, Arlington
PhotoPass freedom, Peirce College
77. Camera guy, Radford University
Slapped student, University of Portland
Titanic ride, University of Southern California

Injured student, Trinity College
78. Buffet of women, SUNY-Potsdam
Magical tanning lotion, Malone College
Smoking dustpan, Fullerton College
79. Broom fight, University of Los Angeles, San Diego & Oklahoma State, Stillwater
Trash can, University of Tulsa
Custodial freedom, Anderson University
Bathroom use, University of Dayton
Dustpan & broom, University of Texas, Brownsville
80. Free admission, ***
High admission prices, Central Washington University
Busted chair, Luther College
81. Airport monorail, Asbury College
Lagoon parking, University of Utah
Attractive guest, ***
Royal descent, Strayer College
82. Sailor's outfit, California State, Bakersfield
Golf cart, University of Michigan & University of Nevada, Las Vegas
Swimming pool golf cart, Hunter College
Stolen towels, ***
83. Sex toys, Black Hills State University
Tug of war, Maryville College & University of Wisconsin, Green Bay
Donald Duck & Minnie Mouse, University of South Dakota
Donald Duck's party, Idaho State University
Donald Duck's house, Midstate College
84. Mickey Mouse's yacht, SUNY-Buffalo
Tragic divorce, Martin University
Ariel's breasts, Valley City State University
Mistaken autograph, ***
Exhausted Goofy, University of California, Irvine
85. Angry mother, University of Oregon
Kicking Mickey Mouse, University of San Francisco
86. Protein spill (Goofy), California State, Fullerton
Protein Spill (Pluto), ***
Snow White, ***
Tigger, ***
87. Pluto, University of Central Florida
Same sex, University of Nebraska, Lincoln
Valentine's Day, Keystone College
Easter, Allen University
Fourth of July, ***
88. Headless Horseman, Chicago State University
Thanksgiving, University of New Hampshire
Fake snow, California State, Sacramento

New Year's Eve celebration, Caldwell College
Y2K, California State, Northridge
89. College Program Easter eggs, Walsh College
Bags of candy, University of Texas, Austin, California State, San Diego, &
University of West Florida.
89. Headless Horseman, Fairfield University
Christmas tree fire, King College
90. Hurricane ride, University of Portland
Hurricane snow, University of California, Davis
Ride-out drinking, SUNY-Albany
Hurricane weather, Wilkes University
Slumber party, University of North Florida
90. Brainwashed cast members, University of Arizona
Flying mouse ears, University of Nevada, Reno
92. Plane, University of California, Los Angeles
Twin towers, SUNY-Brockport
Learned a lot, SUNY-Buffalo
Terrorist ride, University of South Carolina, Union
Selena and Los Dinos, ***
93. Steve Young, Kansas State University
O.J. Simpson, University of Florida
Tony Hawk, Arizona State University
Tiger Woods, University of Montana, Western
Brittany Spears, University of Nebraska, Lincoln
Wayne Brady, University of Central Florida & University of Southern
California
Ravone Symone, ***
Michael Flatley, University of Maryland, Eastern Shore
George Foreman, University of Massachusetts, Boston
Celebrities, University of Nebraska, Lincoln
95. Co-exist, University of California, Davis
Long breaks, ***
Snitch, University of Minnesota, Duluth
96. Peter Pan autograph, ***
Mickey hands, Wofford College
Spilled popcorn, Shorter College
Spectromagic, ***
97. Free admission, ***
Mickey Mouse encounter, University of California, Los Angeles
Bigger castle, University of Arkansas, Little Rock
Haunted Mansion, Andrews University
98. Pirates of the Caribbean, Baldwin-Wallace College
Thunderstorm, Miles College
Hot dogs, ***

Chapter Five
Page

MOUSECATRAZ

Twelve cases of beer, SUNY-Oneonta
Sneaking in students, ***
117. Drugs, ***
Gasoline, University of California, Berkeley
Terminated for under-aged drinking, ***
Profanity, SUNY-Albany
Thunderstorms, Southern Vermont College
118. Dynamic bus vomit, Midwestern State University
Student driving Dynamic bus, ***
Dynamic bus trip to post office, ***
119. Lost driver, University of New Mexico
Sea World, Bard College
Broken down bus, Westminster College
Death trap, ***
Cockroach, University of California, San Diego
120. Being late, North Central University
English, Idaho State University
Crazy drivers, ***
Death, ***
Bus explosion, ***
Counseling, University of Denver
121. Water balloon fight with security, University of the District of Columbia
Water balloon fight, California State, Sacramento
Frisbee dishes, SUNY-Buffalo
Bare butt roommates, California State, Fullerton
Flashing students, University of Delaware
122. Apartment fort, Santa Clara University
Outside video games, Texas A&M, Galveston
Bathroom bodies, ***
Pillow fight, Virginia State University
Mattress rides, ***
Duct tape prank, University of Nebraska, Lincoln
123. Saran wrapped toilet, University of Southern California
Popcorn pillowcase, Penn State, York
Caution tape, Oklahoma City University
Toilet paper, Southwestern University
Jelly in bed, University of Miami
124. Dish soap laundry, Texas State, Lamar
Excessive laundry soap, University of Nevada, Las Vegas
Washing machine abuse, University of Maryland, College Park
First time laundry, California State, Fresno
125. Stolen clothes, University of Colorado, Boulder
Distracted student, Easter Illinois University
Sunscreen, Indiana University, East

Thunderstorm, ***
126. 3:00 A.M. swim, ***
Broken windshield, Minnesota State, Winona
Basketball game, SUNY-Plattsburgh
Grilled bird, California State, Chico
127. Volleyball brawl, University of Houston, Downtown
Basketball tournament, University of New York, Queens College
Pond swim, University of North Carolina, Chapel Hill
Alligator, University of Sioux Falls
128. Shaving cream, SUNY- Buffalo
Cases of Budweiser, University of Richmond
Vomiting student, ***
Early Release, University of California, San Diego
Pleasure Island body shots, University of Wisconsin, Parkside
129. Monopoly, California State, Chico
Passed out roommate, University of Texas, Austin
Vomiting manager, ***
Beer bong, Washington State, Vancouver
Off-site parties, ***
Threesome, University of Southern California
130. Roommate sex, ***
Locked bedroom, University of Illinois, Chicago
Mistaken sex, *** (name, John, used in dialogue was asked to be fictitious)
Cheating student, Delaware State University
 Nameless lovers, ***
131. Slashed tires, ***
Lisa, University of Denver
Volleyball sex, University of the District of Columbia
Laundry room sex, ***
Wounded cat, ***
132. Locked bedroom, SUNY, Brockport
Bus sex, University of Nevada, Reno
Religious student, ***
Shy student, University of San Francisco
Pleasure Island student, ***
133. Group orgy, SUNY-Buffalo State
Hot tub STD's, University of South Carolina, Columbia
Dumping boyfriend, Averett College
Vista Way Baby, SUNY-Buffalo
Vista Way Sex, University of Wyoming
Kitchen sex, ***
134. Clapping student, Brooks College
Making out, University of Texas, Dallas
138. Living experience, University of California, Los Angeles

Chapter Six
Page
140. Communications course, Central Washington University
141. Incorrectly spelled name, ***
Disney Experiential course, University of Richmond
142. Disney Hospitality course, Western Oregon University
Disney Human Resources Management, University of Montana, Western
143. Disney Corporate Analysis course, University of Maryland, Baltimore
Disney Creativity & Innovation course, University of Maryland, Baltimore
Disney Organizational Leadership Course, University of Washington, Tacoma
144. Marketing plan, University of Hawaii, Manoa
Disney Exploration Series, University of Northern Colorado
145. Excited student, California State, Fullerton
146. Thunderstorm, University of Arkansas, Pine Bluff
Pink thong, SUNY-Buffalo
Nametags, Austin College
Belt, Salem State College
Course description, University of California, Davis
Signed roll sheet, ***
147. Theme park call-in, University of Michigan, Dearborn
STD, ***
Hung over, University of Missouri, Kansas City
Grandmother died, University of South Carolina, Upstate
148. Late assignments, Penn State, Berks
"F" paper, ***
Sex paper, University of Sioux Falls
149. Snoring student, University of District of Columbia
Nightmare, Radford University
Tired student, ***
Under the table sleep, Brigham Young University
Closet sleep, Texas A&M University, Commerce
On-line essay, South Dakota State University
150. Copying test answers, ***
Professor answering cell phone, California State, San Diego
Interrupted lecture, University of New Haven
151. Six-figure job, Sierra College
Useless degree, University of Hartford
Framed Mouster's, University of Portland
152. Certified to quack, California State, San Diego
Mouster's vs. Master's, University of Georgia, Fort Valley
Networking, ***
Guest Service Manager, ***

225

Mouse ears, University of California, Davis
Graduation ceremony, ***
Pursuing career, West Virginia University
Blank paper, University of Kentucky
Female manager, ***
176. Come back anytime, ***
Vomit, ***
Don't come back, University of Washington, Tacoma
Haunted Mansion costume, University of West Alabama
Borrowing wardrobe, University of Sioux Falls
177. Pirates' costume, University of Phoenix
Space Mountain costume, University of Wisconsin, Green Bay
Main Street cash register, University of Maryland, College Park
Company vehicle, California State, Sacramento
Stolen dust, ***
Company stationary, ***
178. Star Tours costume, SUNY-Purchase
Risking on last day, University of California, Irvine
Program not for him, Bowie State University
Poisoned cookie, University of California, Los Angeles
Dumped girlfriend, SUNY-Buffalo
179. University of California, Los Angeles
Magical place, University of San Francisco
Missed Disney, University of Nebraska, Omaha
Missed girlfriend, University of the Southwest
180. $100, ***
Spotless apartment, Long Island University, Brooklyn
Used condom, East Tennessee State University
Clean bathroom, University of Wyoming
Exploding suitcase, University of Charleston
Thrown suitcase, California State, San Diego
181. Broken television, Indiana University, South Bend
Vacuum cleaners, Kansas State University
Tightly packed van, Plymouth State University
Sad day, University of Texas, Dallas
Cried all day, ***
Last good-bye, Delaware State University
Checking-out process, California State, Chico
182. Didn't understand, Colorado State University
Memories, Arizona State University, West Campus
183. Re-adjusting, California State, Sacramento
Pleasure Island, University of South Dakota
Disney point on campus, University of California, Davis
Disney point directions, Arkansas State University
Disney Speak, Michigan State University

About the Authors

Wesley Jones has worked for prominent organizations that include The Walt Disney Company, Six Flags Theme Parks, and Target Corporation. He earned his Master of Arts and Master of Science degrees from the University of San Francisco. He earned his "Ducktorate" degree in Organizational Leadership from the Disney College Program. He's currently working on his third book.

Michael Esola, contributing author, has worked for prominent organizations that include the Oakland Athletics Baseball organization, the San Jose Sabercats of the Arena Football League, and the San Francisco Tennis Club. He earned his Bachelor of Arts and Master of Arts degrees from the University of San Francisco. He's currently working on his third book.

Now Available

You Have A College Degree, Now What?

The transition between college to the real world can be challenging and mystifying. It is this unknown journey that can leave individuals in a position where recovery may never be possible. This book will help readers theorize, strategize, and execute for a future that many college graduates hope to obtain.

By Michael Esola & Wesley Jones
(Softcover $14.95)

Now Available in Bookstores

More Information

Is your organization stuck? Need a boost in productivity and morale? Want to ensure that your education and experience are working for you? Visit www.MantraHospitality.com for creative solutions that can help your organization's most valuable asset succeed...People.

CPSIA information can be obtained at www.ICGtesting.com
Printed in the USA
LVOW040739301011

252663LV00002B/61/P